New York Giants Football

By The Numbers

New York Giants Football

By The Numbers

Researched by Tom P. Rippey III

Paul F. Wilson & Tom P. Rippey III, Editors

Kick The Ball, Ltd

Lewis Center, Ohio

By The Numbers Books by Kick The Ball, Ltd

College Football

Ohio State
Buckeyes

Pro Football

New York	New York
Giants	Jets

Pro Baseball

Boston	New York
Red Sox	Yankees

Visit us online at www.ByTheNumberBook.com

This book is dedicated to our families and friends for your unwavering love, support, and your understanding of our pursuit of our passions. Thank you for everything you do for us and for making our lives complete.

New York Giants Football: By The Numbers;
First Edition 2011

Published by
Kick The Ball, Ltd
8595 Columbus Pike, Suite 197
Lewis Center, OH 43035
www.ByTheNumberBook.com

Edited by: Paul F. Wilson & Tom P. Rippey III
Designed and Formatted by Paul F. Wilson
Researched by: Tom P. Rippey III

For information on ordering this book in bulk at reduced prices, please email us at pfwilson@bythenumberbook.com.

International Standard Book Number: 978-1-61320-032-2

Printed and Bound in the United States of America

10 9 8 7 6 5 4 3 2 1

Table of Contents

About Kick The Ball, Ltd *By The Numbers* Books

"By The Numbers" books, articles, magazine features, etc. come in many formats. Most are done in pure chronological order, some match numbers in logical strings or related natural progressions within a category, and still others follow no easily discernable pattern at all.

As you turn the pages of this book, you will notice that we have categorized the numbers based on either the **final or final two digits** of each number. For example, you would find the year 1901 on page 1. The year 1910 would therefore be found on page 10, and so on.

In researching and compiling this book we found that to maintain our desired structure of a 1-100 grouping, this methodology would be necessary. Categorizing numbers 1-100 allows the reader to more quickly reference any given number based on the last digit or two, and gives us the ability to organize the data in exactly 100 pages.

This book is not meant to be exhaustive. Each researcher is given latitude to include a limited number of items they feel are particular important or interesting for each number. Additionally, other supportive or background numbers may be included with the primary number being presented. We do this to add depth to the information you are presented.

You will also notice **Featured Figure** sections spread throughout the pages of this book. These special sections include random, but interesting, information on a number relating to a particular moment or performance in team history.

All information in this book is valid
as of the end of the
2010 season.

New York Giants

○○○ • • • ——————————————— **1**

F
O
O
T
B
A
L
L

The first game in Giants franchise history took place on Oct. 11, 1925, against the Providence Steam Rollers. New York lost the game 0-14.

The Giants won their first game in franchise history on Nov. 1, 1925. They beat the Cleveland Bulldogs 19-0 in the fourth game of the season.

On Sept. 12, 2010, the Giants hosted the first game in the newly built Meadowlands Stadium. Since the Giants share this stadium with the Jets, NFL Commissioner Roger Goodell flipped a coin to determine which team would host the home opener. Not only did the Giants win the coin toss, but they also won the game, beating the Carolina Panthers 31-18.

Bob Folwell was the Giants' first head coach. That inaugural season was Folwell's only season as an NFL head coach.

The Giants played the New York Jets for the first time on Nov. 1, 1970. The Giants won the game 22-10.

New York drafted offensive lineman Art Lewis with the 9th overall pick in the NFL's inaugural draft in 1936. Lewis played one season with the Giants.

The Giants retired jersey #1 in 1935 in honor of Ray Flaherty. He served seven seasons as a Giants assistant coach (1928-29, 1931-35). This was the first jersey retired in NY history.

By The Numbers

——————————————— • • • ○○○

New York Giants

F
O
O
T
B
A
L
L

The Giants played the College All-Stars two times in franchise history. New York won both matchups, 9-0 in 1939 and 22-12 in 1957. The 1939 win by the Giants snapped a three-game winning streak by the College All-Stars. This preseason game was played annually from 1934-76; however, no game was played in 1974 due to an NFL strike. The game matched up the NFL Champion from the previous season against the College All-Stars. Although the Giants were NFL Champions in 1934, they did not participate in the 1935 game. Instead, the NFL representative was the Chicago Bears, runners-up to New York from the previous season.

In 1949, Giants running back Gene Roberts led the NFL in scoring with 102 points. For the season, Roberts had nine rushing touchdowns and eight receiving touchdowns.

Giants quarterback Jeff Rutledge started four games in 1983 and averaged 302 passing yards per game, the highest among players that have started more than one game in a season.

Erich Barnes returned an interception 102 yards against the Cowboys on Oct. 15, 1961, the longest interception return in Giants history and tied for fifth longest in NFL history.

The only points scored in the second quarter of Super Bowl XXI were when Giants defender George Martin tackled John Elway in the end zone for a safety.

By The Numbers

──────────── ● ● ● ○ ○ ○

New York Giants

○○○ ••• ─────────────────── ③

F
O
O
T
B
A
L
L

Three Giants have been named Super Bowl MVP: Phil Simms, Super Bowl XXI; Ottis Anderson, Super Bowl XXV; and Eli Manning, Super Bowl XLII.

New York has had just three coaches that lasted one season or less. Bob Folwell led the team to a record of 8-4 in 1925, Doc Alexander led the team to a record of 8-4 in 1926 and Benny Friedman coached the Giants to two victories in 1930.

Jim Thorpe, arguably the most versatile athlete in history, played three games for the Giants in 1925.

Only three times has a Giants quarterback started all 16 games in a season and had a losing record: Dave Brown in 1995 and 1996 and Kerry Collins in 2001.

Jim Katcavage scored three safeties for the Giants from 1956-68, a team career record.

The most field goals made of 50 or more yards in a season is three. Three Giants players share this record: Jay Feely (2005), Steve Christie (2004) and Joe Danelo (1981).

New York's away jersey has three stripes on the sleeve. Stripes were removed from the home jersey in 2000.

Three Giants players have been named Pro Bowl MVP: Frank Gifford in 1959, Sam Huff in 1961 and Phil Simms in 1986.

••• ○○○

By The Numbers

New York Giants

○ ○ ○ • • • ———————————————— ─ 4 ─

F
O
O
T
B
A
L
L

A Giants quarterback has thrown for 4,000 or more yards in a season four times: Phil Simms in 1984, Kerry Collins in 2002 and Eli Manning in 2009 and 2010.

NY has played in four NFC Championship Games. The Giants are undefeated when playing in this playoff game.

The Giants have played in four Super Bowls (XXI, XXV, XXXV and XLII) and are 3-1 in those matchups.

Y.A. Tittle had a quarterback rating of 104.8 in 1963, the highest single-season rating among Giant quarterbacks with 100 or more attempts. He completed 221 of 367 passes for 3,145 yards, 36 touchdowns and 14 interceptions.

The Giants appeared in the playoffs a team record four consecutive seasons from 2005-08.

New York has trailed at halftime in each of the team's four Super Bowl appearances.

In 1991 Rodney Hampton became the fourth Giants player to rush for 1,000 yards in a season. He gained 1,059 yards on 256 attempts.

New York retired jersey #4 in 1940 in honor of running back Tuffy Leemans. He played for New York from 1936-43 and accumulated 3,142 career rushing yards, 2,324 passing yards, 442 receiving yards and 16 touchdowns.

By The Numbers

• • • ○ ○ ○

New York Giants

○ ○ ○ • • • ─────────────────── ─(5)─

F
O
O
T
B
A
L
L

Giants head coaches have been named NFL Coach of the Year by the Associated Press five times: Allie Sherman, 1961 and 1962; Bill Parcells, 1986; Dan Reeves, 1993; and Jim Fassel, 1997.

Ray Poole recovered five fumbles in 1950. This Giants record was matched by Ernie Jones in 1978.

Amani Toomer surpassed the 1,000-yard mark in receiving yards five consecutive seasons from 1999-03.

Y.A. Tittle completed 27 of 39 passes for 505 yards and seven touchdowns with no interceptions in a 49-34 win against the Washington Redskins on Oct. 28, 1962.

Michael Strahan started in 205 regular-season games, a Giants career record. He ranks 51st of all time in the NFL for this category.

Giants kicker Matt Bahr made a 42-yard field goal as time expired in the 1990 NFC Championship Game against the 49ers. The field goal, Bahr's fifth of the game, gave the Giants a 15-13 win. His other field goals were from 28, 42, 46 and 38 yards, and accounted for all of New York's points.

New York lost five fumbles in the 1958 Eastern Conference Playoff Game, a Giants record for most fumbles lost in a postseason game.

By The Numbers

───────────────────── • • • ○ ○ ○

New York Giants

F
O
O
T
B
A
L
L

Six of the Giants' eight wins in its inaugural season were shutouts.

Carolina Panthers running back Jonathan Stewart rushed for 206 yards against the Giants on Dec. 27, 2009. He is the last player to gain 200 or more rushing yards against New York.

Giants kicker Don Chandler led the NFL in scoring in 1963 with 106 points. For the season, Chandler made 18 field goals and 52 PATs.

New York kicker Dave Jennings led the NFL six seasons in total punt yardage, a team record for leading the league in this category.

The last time the Giants went undefeated in the preseason was in 2006.

New York played in six playoff games from 1939-50, losing each one. This is a team record for consecutive playoff losses. The Giants scored a combined 33 points in those games and allowed 138.

Leon Bright had 106 punt returns for the Giants from 1981-83. He did not fair catch a single punt during those seasons.

The Giants have finished first in the NFC East six times since 1970: 1986, 1989, 1990, 1997, 2000 and 2005.

By The Numbers

New York Giants

○ ○ ○ • • • ———————————————— 7

F
O
O
T
B
A
L
L

New York has won a total of seven NFL titles: four NFL Championships (1927, 1934, 1938 and 1956) and three Super Bowl Titles (XXI, XXV and XLII).

Giants running back Kink Richards led the NFL in 1933 in touchdowns scored with seven.

The Giants have an all-time record of 7-4-3 on Thanksgiving Day for a .607 winning percentage.

Kerry Collins recovered seven of his own fumbles in 2001, a Giants season record.

New York's all-time record against the Pittsburgh Steelers in the regular season is 44-28-3, for a winning percentage of .607.

The NY head coaching tenure for both Jim Fassel and Jim Lee Howell lasted just seven years. They are tied for fourth for the longest tenure as Giants head coach.

The Giants beat the NFC's No. 1 seed Dallas Cowboys 21-17 in the 2007 Divisional Playoffs, the first time an NFC No. 1 seed had been defeated in the divisional round under the current playoff format.

NY retired Mel Hein's jersey #7 in 1963. Hein played center and linebacker for the Giants from 1931-45. He was named NFL MVP in 1938 and set team records for service and games played.

By The Numbers

• • • ○ ○ ○

New York Giants

8

F
O
O
T
B
A
L
L

New York has played the Chicago Bears eight times in the postseason, the most against any NFL team. The Giants are 3-5 against the Bears in those matchups.

The Giants have played in the NFC Wild Card Game eight times: 1984, 1985, 1993, 1997, 2002, 2005, 2006 and 2007. New York is 4-4 in those games.

Giants quarterback Charlie Conerly averaged 8.8 yards per completion in 1959, a single-season record among quarterbacks with 100 or more attempts.

Pete Gogolak made eight PATs against the Philadelphia Eagles on Nov. 26, 1972, a team single-game record.

Y.A. Tittle attempted 1,308 passes during his Giants career. He averaged eight yards per attempt, the highest among players with 250 or more career attempts.

The Giants faced the Cleveland Browns in the 1958 Eastern Division Playoff Game. New York handed the Browns two losses during the regular season. In the playoff game, the Giants outgained the Browns 317-86 yards and won the game 10-0. Jim Brown, the league's leading rusher was held to just eight yards on seven carries. Frank Gifford and Alex Webster combined for 157 rushing yards for the Giants. The sole touchdown of the game was scored on a lateral from Gifford to Charlie Conerly in the first quarter.

By The Numbers

• • • ○ ○ ○

New York Giants

F
O
O
T
B
A
L
L

Lawrence Taylor was named First-Team All-Pro nine times (1981-89).

Howie Livingston led the NFL in interceptions in 1944, the first Giant to lead the league in this category. The last Giant to lead this category was Willie Williams in 1968.

Antonio Pierce was credited with 109 total tackles in 2006. He is the last Giants player to record 100 or more total tackles in a season.

Joe Danelo made nine career field goals of 50 or more yards, a Giants record. Brad Daluiso is second on the list with six.

New York won nine straight games against the Philadelphia Eagles from Oct. 16, 1938, through Nov. 8, 1942. This is a team record for consecutive wins against the Eagles.

The Giants gained a team record 609 total yards against the New York Yankees in 1950.

NY led the Minnesota Vikings 19-3 at halftime in the 1997 Wild Card Playoffs. At the two-minute warning, the Giants led by nine points. However, the defense gave up a touchdown and field goal and lost 22-23.

The Browns attempted nine passes, completing three for 43 yards, in the 1950 American Conference Playoff. All three are postseason records for the fewest by an NY opponent.

By The Numbers

• • • ○ ○ ○

New York Giants

○ ○ ○ • • • ─────────────────── ─(**10**)─

F
O
O
T
B
A
L
L

New York has had three consecutive 10-win seasons two times: 1961 (10-3), 1962 (12-2), 1963 (11-3); and 1988 (10-6), 1989 (12-4), 1990 (13-3).

Lawrence Taylor played in 10 Pro Bowls as a Giant (1981-90), more than any other player.

New York's first 10-win season happened in 1927 when the team finished 11-1-1 for a .885 winning percentage.

The Giants failed to record a 10-win season in both the 1940s and 1970s.

Frank Gifford scored a touchdown in 10 consecutive games spanning the 1957-58 seasons. This is a team record for the most consecutive games scoring a touchdown.

New York's all-time record against the Minnesota Vikings in the regular season is 9-13, for a winning percentage of .410.

New York won its first NFL Championship in 1927. The team posted 10 shutouts in 13 games and outscored opponents 197-20.

Bill Paschal recorded 10 rushing touchdowns in 1943. This would stand as New York's single-season record for 43 years.

By The Numbers

NY had 10 interceptions in 2003, a team record for the fewest interceptions in a season.

─────────────── • • • ○ ○ ○

New York Giants

○ ○ ○ • • • ──────────── ⊕11⊕

F
O
O
T
B
A
L
L

NY drafted running back Ron Dayne out of the University of Wisconsin with the 11th overall pick of the 2000 NFL Draft. This is the last time NY drafted a running back in the first round.

Phil Simms attempted 311 passes and threw just four interceptions in 1990. His .128 interceptions per attempt percentage is the lowest of any Giants quarterback with 100 or more attempts in a season.

Otto Schnellbacher recorded 11 interceptions in 1951. This Giants single-season record was matched by Jimmy Patton in 1958.

Brad Maynard punted 111 times in 1997, a Giants record for the most punts in a season. His total places him third on the NFL's record list for this category.

New York outgained the Philadelphia Eagles by 31 total yards in the 2008 NFC Championship Game, but lost the game 11-23.

New York retired Phil Simms' jersey #11 at halftime of a Monday Night Football Game against the Dallas Cowboys on Sept. 4, 1995.

Featured Figure

NY is undefeated at home against the Cincinnati Bengals (3-0), Houston Texans (1-0), Jacksonville Jaguars (2-0) and Kansas City Chiefs (4-0).

By The Numbers

• • • ○ ○ ○

New York Giants

(12)

F
O
O
T
B
A
L
L

Bill Paschal scored 12 touchdowns his rookie season in 1943, 10 rushing and two receiving. As a team, the Giants only had 22 offensive touchdowns. Paschal's total set a then NFL rookie scoring record and led the league that season. He also led the league in touchdowns scored in 1944 with nine, and is the only Giant to have led the NFL in this category more than once.

Allie Sherman coached the Giants for 112 games. He led the team to a record of 57-51-4 from 1961-68, for a .528 winning percentage. In 1969 Sherman was dismissed due to a lack of success after the departures of Y.A. Tittle and Frank Gifford. He is a member of the Jewish Sports Hall of Fame and worked as a pro-football analyst with ESPN during the 1980s and early 1990s.

The Giants only attempted 12 passes against the Chicago Bears in the 1934 NFL Championship Game. This is a NY postseason record for the fewest attempts in a game.

New York has finished the regular season with 12 wins in 1962, 1989, 2000 and 2008.

Featured Figure

The Giants beat the Pro All-Stars 13-10 on Jan. 15, 1939. This was the first Pro Bowl in NFL history. At the time, the league's champion from the previous year played the All-Stars from the other teams.

By The Numbers

•••○○○

New York Giants

○ ○ ○ • • •

F
O
O
T
B
A
L
L

Phil Simms passed for 513 yards against the Cincinnati Bengals on Oct. 13, 1985. This is the Giants' record for most passing yards in a single game. NY lost the game 30-35. This was Simms' second-consecutive game with 400 or more passing yards. He threw for 432 yards in a 29-30 loss against the Dallas Cowboys the previous week. The 945 yards passing in two-consecutive games is also a franchise record.

Giants wide receiver Homer Jones led the NFL in receiving touchdowns and total touchdowns scored in 1967. He recorded 13 receiving touchdowns and one rushing.

Harry Carson was a linebacker for NY his entire 13-year NFL career. In 1976 he was a fourth-round draft pick from South Carolina State. The nine-time Pro Bowler was enshrined into the Pro Football Hall of Fame in 2006.

Dave Brown led the Giants to a 5-11 record in 1995 for a .313 winning percentage, the worst among all New York quarterbacks who have started 16 games in a season.

The Giants punted the ball 13 times against the Chicago Bears in the 1933 NFL Championship Game. This is the Giants record for the most punts in a postseason game.

By The Numbers

• • • ○ ○ ○

New York Giants

○ ○ ○ • • • —————————————— ⊕ (14)

F
O
O
T
B

NY won 14 regular-season games in 1986, a franchise season record. They allowed just 236 points for the season and beat teams by an average of 8.4 points-per-game, both categories ranked second in the NFL that season. Each of the two losses came on the road, the first was a 28-31 loss to the Dallas Cowboys in Week 1 and the second was a 12-17 loss to the Seattle Seahawks in Week 7.

A
L
L

Giants running back Ron Johnson had 1,514 yards from scrimmage in 1970, the most in the NFL. Johnson had 1,027 yards rushing and 487 receiving. He also led the league that season in rushing attempts with 263.

The worst lost the Giants suffered in their first season was by 14 points. New York suffered the loss of 0-14 twice in 1925, against the Providence Steam Rollers and the Frankford Yellow Jackets.

Emlen Tunnell gained 2,214 yards on punt returns during his Giants career. This would stand as the team record for 37 years.

New York has an all-time regular-season record of 18-17 against current teams in the AFC East for a winning percentage of .514.

The Giants retired Y.A. Tittle's jersey #14 in 1965. He played for NY from 1961-64. In 1963, Tittle led the league in the following passing categories: completions, attempts, yards and touchdowns.

By The Numbers

• • • ○ ○ ○

New York Giants

15

F
O
O
T
B
A
L
L

New York held spring training camp at the University of Albany for 15-consecutive years from 1996-2010, the team's longest consecutive training site at one location in franchise history. Due to limited training time following a league lockout in 2011, training camp was held at Timex Performance Center located near MetLife Stadium.

Lawrence Taylor played in 15 postseason games with the Giants, a team record. There are several players tied for second on the list with 11 postseason games.

Three players have played 15 years with the Giants: Michael Strahan, Phil Simms and Mel Hein. These players are tied for longest service with New York.

Brandon Jacobs scored 15 rushing touchdowns in 2008. He is one of only two Giants players to record 15 or more rushing touchdowns in a season.

Earl Morrall averaged 15.8 yards per completion in 1965 and Fran Tarkenton averaged 15.1 in 1967. They join Y.A. Tittle as the only Giants quarterbacks to average more than 15 yards per completion in a single season.

Phil Simms averaged 15.7 pass completions per game during his NFL career.

Featured Figure

New York is one of just five NFL teams with no official mascot.

By The Numbers

New York Giants

FOOTBALL

Frank Gifford's jersey #16 was retired by the New York Giants in 2000, the most recent of any Giants retired jersey number. He played for New York from 1952-64. Gifford has the unique distinction of making the Pro Bowl as a defensive back and running back.

Phil Simms fumbled 16 times in 1985, his career high for a season. This set a Giants record that has since been broken. Simms' total also led the NFL in the category that season.

Michael Strahan played in 216 games with the Giants. This is a team record for career service.

A new team began NFL play in 1967, the New Orleans Saints. With 16 teams, the league split into four divisions. New York was added to the Century Division along with the Cleveland Browns, St. Louis Cardinals and Pittsburgh Steelers.

Y.A. Tittle averaged 16.1 yards per completion in 1962. This is a Giants single-season record.

Tiki Barber averaged 116.3 rushing yards per game in 2005, a Giants single-season record. Barber's 103.9 rushing yards per game in 2006 is second in NY history.

In 1934, Giants player Red Badgro led the NFL in receptions with 16.

By The Numbers

New York Giants

○ ○ ○ • • •

F
O
O
T
B
A
L
L

The 2011 season marks Bob Papa's 17th year as the radio play-by-play voice of the Giants.

The Giants failed to appear in the playoffs from 1964-80. This 17-year drought is the team's longest absence from the playoffs in franchise history.

The Giants have had 17 head coaches in franchise history.

Brian Mitchell gained 1,117 kickoff return yards in 2003. He ranks second on New York's all-time list and was the first Giants player to surpass 1,000 kickoff yards in a season.

New York had a 25-player roster in 1937. Seventeen of those players were rookies.

The Giants and Redskins faced off in the 1986 NFC Championship Game. New York won the coin toss and decided to kick off because of the swirling 35 mph winds at Giants Stadium, a critical decision. After the Redskins were unable to move the ball, the first punt of the game went just 23 yards and the Giants scored on a Raul Allegre field goal on the ensuing drive. Once again, a short punt on the next Washington possession gave the Giants the ball on the Redskins' 38-yard line. This time, however, the Giants scored on a Phil Simms touchdown pass to Lionel Manuel. NY went on to win 17-0.

By The Numbers

• • • ○ ○ ○

New York Giants

○ ○ ○ • • • ⎯⎯⎯⎯⎯⎯⎯⎯⎯⎯⎯⎯⎯ (**18**)

F
O
O
T
B
A
L
L

The Giants gained 518 total yards (138 rushing, 380 passing) against the Minnesota Vikings in the 2000 NFC Championship game, a NY record for most yards gained in a postseason game. New York limited the Vikings to 114 total yards and won the game 41-0.

New York gained 2,518 rushing yards as a team in 2008. This is a team single-season record. Notable rushers that season were: Brandon Jacobs with 1,089 yards; Derrick Ward with 1,025 yards; and Ahmad Bradshaw with 355 yards.

Joe Danelo kicked a successful field goal in 18 consecutive games, a New York record. Danelo's total broke the record of 14 consecutive made field goals set by Pat Summerall.

New York faced the Philadelphia Eagles in the 1981 Wild Card Playoffs, the Giants' first postseason appearance in 18 years. NY jumped out to a 20-0 lead in the first quarter after two touchdown passes by Scott Brunner and a fumble recovered in the end zone by Mark Haynes. The Giants led 27-7 at halftime and held on for a 27-21 win, the team's first postseason victory in 23 years.

The Rams recorded 18 first downs through the air against the Giants in the 1989 NFC Divisional Playoffs. This is a NY record for the most passing first downs allowed in the postseason.

By The Numbers

• • • ○ ○ ○

New York Giants

○ ○ ○ • • • ───────────── ⑲

F O O T B A L L

Defensive end Jim Katcavage recovered 19 fumbles during his Giants career, a team record.

New York's all-time record against the San Francisco 49ers in the regular season is 14-13, for a winning percentage of .519.

Pete Gogolak attempted 219 field goals during his Giants career. This is a team career record.

In 1967, the Giants allowed the Green Bay Packers to gain 19 first downs. This single-game record for the most first downs allowed was matched in 1978 by the Buffalo Bills.

Featured Figure

The 2004 NFL Draft ended with one of the biggest trade deals of the decade. Prior to the draft, Eli Manning expressed his dislike with the idea of playing in San Diego. The Chargers had the first pick overall and wanted to draft a franchise quarterback. San Diego stubbornly drafted Manning anyway. Three picks later the Giants drafted Philip Rivers. The two would soon be swapping jerseys. The Giants traded Rivers, their third round pick of 2004 and their first round pick of 2005 in exchange for Eli Manning. The Chargers used those picks to draft Nate Kaeding in 2004 and Shawne Merriman in 2005. Although Manning's passer rating, completion percentage and touchdown to interception ratio may not be as good as Rivers', he does posses one thing that eludes Rivers – a Super Bowl ring.

By The Numbers

• • • ○ ○ ○

New York Giants

○ ○ ○ ● ● ●

20

F
O
O
T
B
A
L
L

Craig Morton had a .320 winning percentage as a starting quarterback, the lowest among Giants quarterbacks with at least 30 starts. He had a record of 8-25 from 1974-76.

Lawrence Taylor had 20.5 sacks in 1986, the most in the NFL that season.

An NFL playoff-game attendance record was set when 48,120 fans attended the 1938 NFL Championship Game between the Giants and Packers, which was held at the Polo Grounds in New York.

New York finished the 1920s with a record of 44-17-5 for a .704 winning percentage, the team's highest winning percentage of any decade.

Eli Manning led the NFL with 20 interceptions in 2007 and with 25 in 2010. He is the only Giants player to have led the league in this category more than once.

Giants receiver Steve Smith gained 1,220 receiving yards in 2009.

The Giants held opponents to a combined 20 points in 1927. This is the team record for the fewest points allowed in a season. Only three opponents scored all season, two teams scored seven points and one six. The Giants shut out the other 10 opponents that season.

By The Numbers

● ● ● ○ ○ ○

New York Giants

○ ○ ○ • • • ─────────────────── ⊕ **21**

F
O
O
T
B
A
L
L

New York's first Super Bowl win came against the Denver Broncos in Super Bowl XXI. The Giants trailed 9-10 at halftime before unleashing 24-unanswered points in the second half. Five different players scored touchdowns for the Giants. Although Elway scrambled for 27 yards, the Giants defense held Denver's running backs to just 25 total yards rushing. The final score was 39-20, New York's first NFL Championship since 1956. Phil Simms was named Super Bowl MVP.

Giants running back Joe Morris led the NFL in 1985 in touchdowns scored with 21. He is the last Giants player to lead the league in this category. His season total is also a Giants single-season record. He broke Bill Paschal's record of 10 rushing touchdowns that was set in 1943.

Zeke Mowatt received a six-yard touchdown pass from Phil Simms in the first quarter of Super Bowl XXI, the Giants' first points of the game.

Giants receiver Ray Flaherty led the NFL with 21 receptions in 1932.

Eli Manning passed for 4,021 yards in 2009 and 4,002 yards in 2010. He is the only Giants quarterback to pass for 4,000 yards twice.

By The Numbers

─────────── • • • ○ ○ ○

New York Giants

○○○•••

F
O
O
T
B
A
L
L

In 1956 Frank Gifford led the NFL with 1,422 yards-from-scrimmage. He finished the season with 819 rushing yards and 603 receiving yards.

Michael Strahan led the NFL in sacks in 2001 with 22.5. He also led the league in 2003 with 18.5. He is the only Giant to have led this category more than once.

Joe Morris gained 122 rushing yards against the Phoenix Cardinals in a 44-7 Giants win on Dec. 4, 1988. This game put Morris over 5,000 career rushing yards with the Giants.

Pete Athas had 22 fair catches on 51 punt returns for 449 yards during his Giants career from 1971-74. He ranks ninth on NY's all-time list for career punt return yards but his average of 8.8 yards per return ranks sixth among those on the list.

The Giants attained quarterback Earl Morrall from the Detroit Lions prior to the 1965 season. He passed for a reputable 2,446 yards and 22 touchdowns that season.

Tiki Barber returned 122 punts for NY. His 1,177 total punt return yards ranks fourth all time in Giants history.

Featured Figure

The Giants held training camp in Superior, Wis., in 1939, 1941-42 and 1946. The team traveled even farther in the 1950s. NY held camp at Willamette University in Salem, Ore.

By The Numbers

•••○○○

New York Giants

(23)

F O O T B A L L

New York's all-time regular-season record against the Dallas Cowboys is 39-56-2, for a winning percentage of .423.

Kerry Collins fumbled the football 23 times in 2001, a single-season Giants record. His total that season set an NFL record for the category. Collins had 11 or more fumbles in three of his five seasons in New York.

Brad Daluiso made 123 field goals during his career with the Giants. He ranks second on New York's all-time list.

New York set a regular-season home-game attendance record when 81,223 fans passed through the turnstiles on Dec. 19, 2010, to see the Giants host the Philadelphia Eagles. NY lost the game 31-38.

New York has an all-time regular-season record of 67-61-5 against current teams in the AFC North for a winning percentage of .523.

The Giants were shut out 0-23 by the Carolina Panthers in the 2005 Wild Card Playoffs. It was just the third NY postseason loss in Giants Stadium history and the fifth time the team had been shut out in team postseason history. The Giants were held to just 132 yards and Eli Manning threw three interceptions and had one lost fumble. Carolina rushed for 223 yards, the second most rushing yards allowed in Giants postseason history.

By The Numbers

• • • ○ ○ ○

New York Giants

(24)

**F
O
O
T
B
A
L
L**

Osi Umenyiora has returned 13 fumbles for a total of 224 fumble return yards, a Giants career record. His total places him third on the NFL's list for this category, just 44 yards behind first place Aeneas Williams.

New York beat the Tampa Bay Buccaneers 24-0 on Sept. 27, 2009. This was the last time the Giants have shut out an opponent.

Emlen Tunnell gained 924 combined yards on kickoff and interception returns in 1924. This was more than the 894 rushing yards gained by the NFL's leading rusher that season.

Rodney Hampton set the Giants' record for career rushing attempts in 1995 when he passed Joe Morris' 1,318 career attempts. Hampton finished his career with 1,824 but was surpassed by Tiki Barber in 2005, who ultimately finished with 2,217 career attempts.

New York allowed 24-unanswered points in a 2002 Wild Card Playoff Game against the San Francisco 49ers. A Matt Bryant field goal with 4:24 left in the third quarter gave the Giants a 38-14 lead. Jeff Garcia led the 49ers back with two touchdown passes, two two-point conversion passes and a touchdown run. Even so, Matt Bryant had a chance to kick a 41-yard game-winning field goal. But the snap was low and an erratic throw by holder Matt Allen fell incomplete.

By The Numbers

• • • ○ ○ ○

New York Giants

○ ○ ○ • • •   25

F
O
O
T
B
A
L
L

Three Giants quarterbacks have thrown 25 interceptions in a season, a team single-season record. Eli Manning threw 25 in 2010, Charlie Conerly in 1953 and Frank Filchock in 1946.

Tiki Barber recovered 25 of his own fumbles during his Giants career, highest among running backs and nine more than Dave Meggett, the running back with the second highest career total.

Phil McConkey had 25 fair catches on punt returns in 1988, a Giants single-season record.

The Giants faced the Buffalo Bills in Super Bowl XXV. Entering the game, NY led the league in fewest points allowed during the regular season, while the Bills led the league in scoring. NY struck first and led 3-0 for a brief period. Buffalo scored the next 12 points: a field goal, touchdown and safety. But the Giants were able to cut the lead with a touchdown pass from Jeff Hostetler to Stephen Baker with less than a minute before halftime. New York's opening possession of the second half consumed more than nine minutes and resulted in a 1-yard Ottis Anderson touchdown run. Following a Thurman Thomas touchdown and a Matt Bahr field goal, the Giants led 20-19, setting up a dramatic finish. Buffalo kicker Scott Norwood missed a game-winning field goal with just seconds remaining, sailing wide right. Ottis Anderson was named Super Bowl MVP after gaining 102-yards rushing on 21 carries and one touchdown.

By The Numbers

• • • ○ ○ ○

New York Giants

○○○ ● ● ●

F
O
O
T
B
A
L
L

Sean Landeta punted 526 times during his career with the Giants from 1985-93, and ranks second on the team's career list. He ranks second all time in the NFL with 1,401 punts during his entire career. He is 312 punts behind former Giants punter Jeff Feagles, who punted 513 times during his seven years with New York.

Pat Summerall made 126 consecutive PATs from 1958-61. This is second best in Giants history and 41 more consecutive PATs than third place Brad Daluiso.

Pete Gogolak made 126 career field goals as a Giant, a team record.

New York's all-time regular-season record against the Philadelphia Eagles is 79-71-2, for a winning percentage of .526.

Clarence Childs returned 126 kickoffs during his four seasons with the Giants. He ranks second on the team's all-time list for this category.

New York has an all-time regular-season record of 209-188-8 against current teams in the NFC East for a winning percentage of .526.

The Rams recorded 26 first downs against the Giants in the 1989 NFC Divisional Playoffs. This is the most allowed in the postseason by NY since 1950.

By The Numbers

● ● ● ○○○

New York Giants

ooo••• ───────────────────────── 27

F
O
O
T
B
A
L
L

One of the most famous games played by the New York Giants was the "Sneakers Game." The temperature was just nine degrees when the Giants hosted the Chicago Bears at the Polo Grounds in 1934. Complicating matters was the sheet of ice that covered the field. Trailing 3-10 at halftime, Giants coach Steve Owen decided to follow the suggestion of a player and get some sneakers for the team to improve traction. After the Bears widened the lead in the third quarter with a successful field goal, nine Giants changed out their cleats for basketball shoes. New York scored 27 unanswered points following the switch and won the game 30-13.

The Giants drafted offensive tackle Roosevelt Brown out of Morgan State in the 27th round of the 1953 NFL Draft. Brown is considered one of the greatest sleeper picks of all time. He played 13 seasons with the Giants and was named to the Pro Bowl nine times and All-NFL eight times. Brown was inducted into the Pro Football Hall of Fame in 1975.

Rocky Thompson averaged 27.2 yards per kickoff return, highest among all Giants players with 40 or more career returns. His career average ranks 8th of all time in the NFL.

Ron Johnson rushed for 1,027 yards in 1970. He is the first 1,000-yard rusher in Giants history.

New York has an all-time regular-season record of 125-112-5 against current AFC teams, for a winning percentage of .527.

By The Numbers

•••ooo

New York Giants

28

F
O
O
T
B
A
L
L

Phil Simms recovered 28 of his own fumbles during his Giants career, a team record. He ranks 28th of all time in the NFL in this category.

After a 4-7-2 finish in 1928, Giants owner Tim Mara fired the head coach and ended the contract of 18 players. The only starter that returned the following season was offensive lineman, and future head coach, Steve Owen.

New York scored 10-unanswered points in the last minute of a game against the Washington Redskins on Nov. 23, 1941. This win secured the Eastern Division title and a trip to the NFL Championship Game against the Chicago Bears, the third matchup between the two teams in the title game. A 16-yard field goal by Giants kicker Ward Cuff evened the game 9-9 in the third quarter. Chicago responded with 28-unanswered points. NY lost the game 9-37 and was outgained 157-389 yards. The game was played two weeks after the bombing of Pearl Harbor.

Phil Simms averaged 28.3 pass attempts per game during his career with the Giants.

Featured Figure

Ward Cuff averaged 5.6 yards per rushing attempt in 1944. This Giants single-season record for the category, it was matched by Eddie Price in 1950, Derrick Ward in 2008 and Brandon Jacobs in 2010.

By The Numbers

● ● ● ○ ○ ○

New York Giants

FOOTBALL

Former Giants owner Tim Mara bought the struggling Detroit Wolverines franchise in 1929 to acquire the rights of rising football star Benny Friedman. Friedman played three seasons with NY and the team nearly won a second championship in his first year. He was inducted into the Pro Football Hall of Fame as a running back in 2005.

Red Badgro scored on a 29-yard pass from Harry Newman in the second quarter of the 1933 NFL Championship Game. The score gave the Giants the lead and were the first points scored in a playoff game in Giants history.

New York's all-time record against the Indianapolis Colts in the regular season is 6-8, for a winning percentage of .429.

The Giants acquired quarterback Fran Tarkenton from the Vikings in 1967. In return, the Vikings received New York's first and second round draft picks in 1967, first round pick in 1968 and second round pick in 1969. Tarkenton's 29 touchdown passes in 1967 helped the Giants rebound from a 1-12-1 record to a 7-7 record.

Lionel Manuel led the team with 1,029 receiving yards in 1988. He was only the third Giants player to surpass 1,000 receiving yards in a season, a mark that wouldn't be surpassed by another Giants player until Amani Toomer in 1999.

By The Numbers

•••ooo

New York Giants

○ ○ ○ ● ● ●

(30)

F
O
O
T
B
A
L
L

The Giants have drafted 30 players from the University of Mississippi, more than from any other school. The last player New York drafted from Ole Miss was defensive end Rodney Lowe in 1989.

Dave Meggett gained a team record 2,230 yards on punt returns during his career with the Giants.

Giants founder Tim Mara turned over ownership to his two sons, Jack and Wellington, in 1930.

New York finished the 1930s with a record of 80-39-8 for a .661 winning percentage.

Matt Bahr scored 30 points for the Giants in postseason games. His scoring total is surpassed only by Brad Daluiso and Ken Strong, who each has a total of 36 postseason points scored.

In 1947, Ken Strong led the Giants in scoring with 30 points. This is the lowest total for the scoring leader since 1936.

Featured Figure

New York has an all-time regular-season record of 440-383-15 against teams currently in the NFC for a winning percentage of .534.

By The Numbers

New York Giants

○ ○ ○ • • • ――――――――――――――――――― (31)

F
O
O
T
B
A
L
L

Y.A. Tittle completed 731 passes for 10,439 yards as a Giants quarterback from 1961-64. His 14.3 yards per completion average is the highest among quarterbacks with 250 or more completions.

Dave Jennings punted 931 times during his career with the Giants from 1974-84, a team career record. He ranks sixth of all time in the NFL with 1,154 punts during his entire career.

Jack Salscheider averaged 31.6 yards per kickoff return in 1949, a Giants single-season record. His average that season ranks 19th best of all time in the NFL.

The Giants finished the 1926 NFL season in seventh place with a record of 8-4-1. Following the end of the season, New York faced off in a game against the Philadelphia Quakers, champions of the American Football League. NY won the game 31-0.

NY signed a contract with center Mel Hein for $150 a game in 1931. They outbid two other teams for his services. Hein played 15 seasons with the Giants and made the Pro Bowl four times and was named First Team All-Pro five times. He was inducted into the Pro Football Hall of Fame in 1963.

NY had 31 passes intercepted in 1983, tied for second most in team history behind the 34 interceptions in 1953.

By The Numbers

• • • ○ ○ ○

New York Giants

○ ○ ○ • • •

F
O
O
T
B
A
L
L

Lawrence Taylor recorded 132.5 sacks during his 13-year career with the Giants. He ranks eighth on the NFL's all-time list for most sacks in a career.

Sean Landeta holds the Giants career record for punt yards in the postseason with 1,832 punt yards.

In the second quarter of the 2000 NFC Divisional Playoffs against the Philadelphia Eagles, Giants defensive back Jason Sehorn returned an interception 32 yards. The Giants won the game 20-10, without scoring a single offensive touchdown.

NY retired Al Blozis' jersey #32 in 1945. Blozis played tackle for the Giants from 1942-44. Soon after the 1944 NFL Championship game, Blozis was sent to France to fight in World War II. He was killed in action six weeks later.

Eli Manning had 3,332 career passing attempts at the end of the 2010 season. This ranks second on the Giants all-time career list for attempts.

Giants quarterback Jack McBride led the NFL in 1932 with 8.2 pass attempts per game.

In 1932, New York end Ray Flaherty led the NFL with 350-receiving yards.

NY allowed the Cowboys to gain 32 first downs in 1978, the second most first downs allowed in team history.

By The Numbers

• • • ○ ○ ○

New York Giants

○ ○ ○ • • • ———————— 33

F
O
O
T
B
A
L
L

The Giants are 7-14 all time in games following a bye week, for a winning percentage of .333.

The NFL split into an Eastern and Western Division prior to the 1933 season. The Giants won the Eastern Division and played the Western Division champion Chicago Bears at Wrigley Field on Dec. 17, 1933. The game marked the NFL's first-ever playoff game. Giants quarterback Harry Newman completed 12 passes for 201 yards and the Giants were winning 21-16 until a 32-yard Chicago run with less than a minute to go put the Bears up for good. New York lost 21-23.

Brad Maynard had 33 punts downed inside the 20-yard line in 1997 and again in 1998. This is a Giants record for the most punts downed inside the 20 within a season.

New York's all-time record against the Kansas City Chiefs in the regular season is 10-2, for a winning percentage of .833.

New York's all-time record against the Baltimore Ravens in the regular season is 1-2, for a winning percentage of .333.

Pete Gogolak made 133 consecutive PATs from 1967-72. This is a New York record.

Phil Simms set a Giants single-season record in 1984 with 533 pass attempts. It would stand until broken by Kerry Collins in 2001.

———————— • • • ○ ○ ○

By The Numbers

New York Giants

○ ○ ○ • • •

F O O T B A L L

Tiki Barber rushed for 234 yards against the Washington Redskins on Dec. 30, 2006, a Giants single-game record. Barber had 23 carries and three touchdowns on the day. His rushing total was 106 more than the combined total for the Redskins.

Most football fans know Frank Gifford for his great Monday Night Football commentary; however, few remember his versatility as a player. In college, Gifford played quarterback, halfback, fullback, punter and place kicker for the Southern Cal Trojans. In 1951 he made Southern Cal's first field goal since 1937. In a showdown with the No. 1 ranked Cal Bears, Gifford had a touchdown pass, 69-yard touchdown run and drove the Trojans to the winning score with less than five minutes to play. He was a first round draft pick by the Giants in 1952, and was named NFL MVP in 1956. In his twelve NFL seasons, Gifford played in eight Pro Bowls and five NFL Championship games. He retired in 1964 after amassing 3,609 yards rushing with 34 touchdowns, 5,434 yards receiving with 43 touchdowns and passed for 823 yards with 14 touchdowns. Not only was he the voice of football for over 20 years, but also one of the last truly multipurpose players.

NY won its first ever NFL Championship Game in 1934. They finished the regular season 8-5 and beat the Chicago Bears 30-13 in the championship game.

By The Numbers

• • • ○ ○ ○

New York Giants

○○○•••─────────────────── 35

F
O
New York has lost their home opener 35 times, most recently in 2007 when the Giants lost 13-35 to the Green Bay Packers.

O
T
B
Ali Haji-Sheikh made 35 field goals in 1983, most in the NFL that season. He is the last Giants player to have led the league in this category. His total set a Giants record that was matched by Jay Feely in 2005.

A
L
L
Eli Manning completed a 13-yard touchdown pass to Plaxico Burress with 35 seconds left in Super Bowl XLII. It was the 12th play of an 83-yard drive. The touchdown pass was the Giants' second of the fourth quarter and put New York up for good, giving the franchise its third Super Bowl title.

New York played the Detroit Lions in the 1935 NFL Championship Game, the Giants' third consecutive appearance in the game. New York's sole score came on a third-quarter, 42-yard pass from Ken Strong to Ed Danowski. The Giants lost 7-26.

New York faced the Baltimore Ravens in Super Bowl XXXV. The Giants offense managed just 152 yards. Although the New York defense played well, limiting the Ravens to 244 total yards, the Giants lost the game 7-34. NY's sole touchdown was the result of a 97-yard kickoff return by Ron Dixon. But the celebration didn't last long. Baltimore's Jermaine Lewis returned the ensuing kickoff 84 yards to put the Ravens back up by 17.

By The Numbers

•••○○○

New York Giants

(36)

F
O
O
T
B
A
L
L

Y.A. Tittle threw 36 touchdown passes in 1963, a Giants single-season record. He also threw 33 touchdowns in 1962. Eli Manning is the only other player to have thrown 30 or more in a season. He threw 31 touchdowns in 2010.

Joe Morris set a Giants single-season record in 1985 with 1,336 rushing yards. The record would stand until broken by himself when he rushed for 1,516 yards in 1986. That record would stand until broken by Tiki Barber in 2004.

Tom Coughlin's first NFL head coaching job in the NFL was with the Jacksonville Jaguars. Including playoffs, he coached the Jaguars a total of 136 games. Coughlin had a regular-season record of 68-60 (.531) and playoff record of 4-4. He was fired following the 2002 season, his third straight losing season with Jacksonville.

Giants quarterback Harry Newman led the NFL with 136 passing attempts in 1933. This would stand as NY's single-season record until 1946.

Tuffy Leemans led the NFL in 1936 with a per-game average of 69.2 rushing yards. He led the league again in 1940 with an average of 47.4.

Featured Figure

New York has an all-time record of 5-5 in the regular season against the Denver Broncos, San Diego Chargers and Tennessee Titans, for a winning percentage of .500.

By The Numbers

● ● ● ○ ○ ○

New York Giants

○ ○ ○ • • •

F
O
O
T
B
A
L
L

The Giants allowed just 137 first downs in 1975, third fewest in franchise history.

Everson Walls returned an interception 37 yards against the Bears in the 1990 NFC Divisional Playoffs. It was his only postseason interception as a Giant, but the longest postseason interception return in NY history.

The Giants' all-time record against the New York Jets in the regular season is 7-4, for a winning percentage of .637.

Frank Leibel caught four passes for 150 yards against the Detroit Lions in 1945. His 37.5 average per reception for the game ranks third of all time in Giants history.

Brad Maynard punted 13 times against the Washington Redskins in 1997 for 537 yards. He ranks second on the Giants all-time list behind Carl Kinscherf's 583 total punt yards against Detroit in 1943.

New York opponents combined for just 182 pass attempts in 1937. This stood as the team single-season record for the fewest attempts until 1963 when opponents combined for 149 pass attempts.

Featured Figure

The Giants have an all-time regular-season record of 626-517-33 for a .546 winning percentage.

By The Numbers

• • • ○ ○ ○

New York Giants

38

F
O
O
T
B
A
L
L

Giants defensive tackle Jim Katcavage led the NFL in fumble return yards in 1961 with 38 yards.

Giants center Mel Hein received the Joe F. Carr Trophy in 1938, given to the league's MVP from 1938-46. This is considered the first NFL MVP Award.

Ken Strong kicked a 38-yard field goal in the 1934 NFL Championship Game against the Chicago Bears at the Polo Grounds on Dec. 9. This was the first field goal in Giants playoff history.

The Giants beat the Green Bay Packers 23-17 in the 1938 NFL Championship Game. The game went back and forth and required a Giants defensive stop as time expired. New York scored nine points off two blocked punts in the first quarter. But Green Bay responded and took a 17-16 lead in the third quarter. Later in the quarter, Hank Soar scored on a 23-yard pass from Ed Danowski to give NY the final lead. This was New York's third NFL Championship.

Harry Newman carried the ball 38 times against Green Bay in 1934. This stood the Giants single-game record for rushing attempts for 60 years. It was broken by Rodney Hampton's 41 attempts against the Rams in 1993.

The Giants lost 20-23 to the Philadelphia Eagles on a 38-yard David Akers field goal as time expired in the 2006 Wild Card Playoffs.

By The Numbers

• • • ○ ○ ○

New York Giants

F
O
O
Eli Manning set a Giants single-season completion record in 2010 with 339. His completion percentage of .629 that season is the highest among Giants quarterbacks with 100 or more attempts in a season.

T
B
A
The Giants lost 0-27 to the Green Bay Packers in the 1939 NFL Championship Game. New York trailed 0-7 at halftime, but the Packers scored 10 points in the third and fourth quarters to secure the title. The Giants managed to gain just seven first downs and 149 yards.

L
L
New York's defense intercepted 39 passes in 1948. This stood as the team's single-season record until 1951 when the current record was set with 41 interceptions.

The Giants completed 339 of 539 pass attempts in 2010.

Featured Figure

Tim Mara, the original owner of the Giants, bought the NFL franchise for $500 in 1925, which is equivalent to $6,500 in 2011 when adjusted for inflation. But the team had problems making money since most football fans preferred the college game. It wasn't until back-to-back games with the Chicago Bears at New York's Polo Grounds to end the season that the team turned a profit. Those games featured former college-great Red Grange. Mara was inducted into the Pro Football Hall of Fame with the class of 1963 as a Founder-Administrator.

By The Numbers

• • • o o o

New York Giants

○○○ •••

F
O
O
T
B
A
L
L

Emlen Tunnell recorded 1,240 interception return yards in his Giants career from 1948-58, a team record. His 1,282 NFL career total ranks fifth of all time.

New York had an all-time record of 2-3 at home in playoff games in the Polo Grounds for a winning percentage of .400.

New York finished the 1940s with a record of 55-47-8 for a .527 winning percentage.

The Giants have an all-time postseason record of 16-24 for a .400 winning percentage.

New York's all-time record against the Buffalo Bills in the regular season is 4-6, for a winning percentage of .400.

The Giants retired Joe Morrison's jersey #40 in 1972. Morrison played for New York from 1959-72. During his 14 years with the team, Morrison spent time playing fullback, halfback, flanker, tight end, split end and defensive back. He gained 7,465 career yards from scrimmage (2,472 rushing, 4,993 receiving) and scored 65 career touchdowns (18 rushing, 47 receiving).

Featured Figure

The Giants played their home games at Shea Stadium in 1975 while Giants Stadium was completed. New York finished the season 2-5 at the Mets' home stadium.

By The Numbers

••• ○○○

New York Giants

○ ○ ○ ● ● ● ──────────────────── **41**

F
O
O
T
B
A
L
L

Michael Strahan recorded 141.5 sacks during his 15-year career with the Giants. He ranks fifth on the NFL's all-time list for most sacks in a career.

Arnie Herber led the Giants with 641 passing yards in 1945. This is the last time the season leading passer had fewer than 1,000 yards.

Jay Feely made .841 of his attempted field goals during his Giants career. This is the highest career percentage among kickers that have 50 or more career attempts. Feely made 58 of 69 attempts.

The Giants lost 3-44 to the San Francisco 49ers in the 1993 NFC Divisional Playoffs. The 41-point differential is the worst loss in New York postseason history.

NY allowed just 41 first downs through the air in 1937, a club record for fewest allowed in a season.

The Giants beat the Minnesota Vikings 41-0 in the 2000 NFC Championship Game. It was only the third time in NY postseason history that the Giants shut out an opponent. New York jumped out to a 34-0 halftime lead. Kerry Collins threw five touchdown passes in the game and passed for 385 yards. The defense held the Vikings to 114 total yards, while the Giants offense gained 518 total yards. In a scoreless fourth quarter, the Giants possessed the ball for the final 12 minutes and 53 seconds.

By The Numbers

● ● ● ○ ○ ○

New York Giants

──────────────── 42

F
O
Ali Haji-Sheikh attempted 42 field goals in 1983. This Giants' single-season record was matched by Jay Feely in 2005.

O
T
B
A
Kerry Collins passed for 342 yards against the 49ers in the 2002 Wild Card Playoff Game and 381 yards against the Vikings in the 2000 NFC Championship Game. He is the only Giants quarterback to pass for 300 or more yards in a postseason game.

L
L
L
The Giants and Redskins faced off in the first game of the 1942 season. New York gained zero first downs compared the Washington's 15, New York gained 1 rushing yard compared to Washington's 120, and New York completed one pass compared to Washington's 12. However, the Giants won the game 14-7. The single pass completion went for a 50-yard touchdown and Neal Adams returned an interception 66 yards for the Giants' second touchdown. Washington shook off the loss and went undefeated the rest of the season, winning the NFL Championship.

Amani Toomer caught a team record 42 passes in the postseason during his career with the Giants.

New York's all-time record against the St. Louis Rams in the regular season is 13-25 (.342).

The Giants retired Charley Conerly's jersey #42 in 1962. He played quarterback for NY from 1948-61. He held the team records for career passing completions (1,418) and passing yards (19,488) at the time of his retirement.

By The Numbers

•••○○○

42

New York Giants

○ ○ ○ • • •

43

F
O
O
T
B
A
L
L

Amani Toomer gained 1,343 yards receiving in 2002, a Giants single-season record. He grabbed 82 receptions and scored eight touchdowns. He averaged 16.4 yards per reception and 83.9 yards per game.

Don Chandler averaged 43.8 yards per punt during his Giants career, a team record among players with 150 or more career punts.

After starting 2-3-1 to start the season in 1943, the Giants won their last four games of the regular season. They met the Washington Redskins in the Eastern Division Playoffs. This was the first time the top two teams in each division faced off in a playoff matchup. New York beat the Redskins 14-10 and 31-7 in the last two games of the regular season but lost 0-28 in the playoffs. New York was outgained 112-296 yards.

Butch Woolfolk carried the ball 43 times against the Eagles in 1983. This is New York's record for the most carries in a game.

New York has an all-time regular-season record of 68-86-5 against current teams in the NFC North for a winning percentage of .443.

Featured Figure

Michael Strahan was named to the 2000s NFL Team of the Decade by the NFL. He was the only Giants player to be named to the list. The All-Decade Team is voted on by the Pro Football Hall of Fame Selection Committee.

By The Numbers

• • • ○ ○ ○

New York Giants

○○○••• ——————————————————— 44

F
O
O
T
B
A
L
L

The Giants defense gave up 44 points to the San Francisco 49ers in the 1993 NFC Division Playoffs, the most points ever allowed by NY in a postseason game. The 49ers outgained the Giants 413 yards to 194. San Francisco running back Ricky Watters set an NFL postseason single-game record with five rushing touchdowns, surprising since the Giants defense gave up just seven rushing touchdowns all season. This game was the last for Giants great Lawrence Taylor, who announced his retirement from football following the game.

New York convinced former Giants player Ken Strong and Packers player Arnie Herber to return from retirement to join the team prior to the 1944 season. Strong had been away from the game for four years. Herber played 11 seasons in Green Bay and retired after the 1940 season. Herber led the Giants with 651 passing yards and Strong was second on the team in scoring with 41 points. Their efforts helped the Giants secure an Eastern Division Championship. New York faced Herber's old team, the Green Bay Packers, in the 1944 NFL Championship Game. This was the third meeting between the two teams in the championship game with each team having won one of the previous matchups. The Giants lost the rubber match 7-14.

Phil Simms set a Giants single-season record in 1984 with 4,044 passing yards. The record would stand until broken by Kerry Collins in 2002.

NY set a team record with 44 takeaways in the 1997 season.

By The Numbers

•••○○○

New York Giants

○ ○ ○ ● ● ●

45

F
O
O
T
B
A
L
L

Despite a promising 34-6 victory in the first game of the season against the Pittsburgh Steelers, New York finished 1945 with a record of 3-6-1 for a winning percentage of .350, which was the franchise's worst record since it began play in 1925.

The Giants recorded 45.0 quarterback sacks in 2010.

Joe Morris scored on a 45-yard rushing attempt against the San Francisco 49ers in the 1986 NFL Playoffs, which broke the record for the longest postseason rush in Giants history set by Ken Strong in 1934. However, Rodney Hampton broke Morris' record with a 51-yard rushing score against the Vikings in the 1993 Wild Card Playoffs.

Dave Jennings punted for 4,445 yards in 1979, the third highest season total in Giants history.

Norm Snead threw 45 interceptions and only 27 touchdown passes in his career with the Giants. His 4,644 career passing yards ranks tenth of all time in team history.

Five players combined for 1,534 passing yards for the Giants in 1945. Arnie Herber led the team with 641 yards and nine touchdown passes.

Featured Figure

The Giants held training camp at Fairleigh Dickson University located in Teaneck, N.J. from 1988-95.

By The Numbers

● ● ● ○ ○ ○

New York Giants

F
O
O
T
B
A
L
L

Pete Gogolak played for New York from 1966-74 and scored 646 points during his Giants career, a franchise career scoring record. He successfully made 268 PATs and 126 field goals on his way to setting this record.

Don Chandler averaged 46.6 yards per punt in 1959, a Giants single-season record among players with 35 or more punts.

Pat Summerall made 46 of 46 PATs in 1961. This is the highest total among Giants kickers who had no misses in a season.

Dave Meggett returned 146 career kickoffs in his career with the Giants. This is a team record.

New York sealed up the Eastern Division in 1946 and played the Chicago Bears in the NFL Championship Game. It was the Giants' eighth appearance in the title game in 14 years, and the fourth against the Bears. A betting scandal broke the day before the game in which Giants quarterback Frankie Filchock and running back Merle Hapes were accused of looking to throw the title game. Hapes was suspended while Filchock was allowed to play. For the game, Filchock completed 9 of 26 passes for 128 yards and six interceptions. He did, however, throw two touchdowns, accounting for all of the Giants' 14 points. NY lost the game 14-24 and Filchock was banned from play by the NFL in 1947. He was reinstated in 1950, playing one game with the Baltimore Colts, the last of his NFL career.

By The Numbers

• • • ○ ○ ○

New York Giants

ooo•••

F
O
O
T
B
A
L
L

Phil Simms attempted a team career record 4,647 passes as a Giant. Simms attempted 400 or more passes in a season seven times in his career. The fewest passes he attempted in seasons in which he played 16 games were 400 in 1993.

The Giants have played the AFC teams a total of 147 times and has a 78-69 record against the conference for a .531 winning percentage.

In 1947 New York started the season 0-7-2 before finishing 2-8-2 for a winning percentage of .250, a new franchise low. The team's 119-point differential for the season ranked last in the league.

NY's all-time record against the Cleveland Browns in the regular season is 19-26-2, for a winning percentage of .447.

New York's all-time record against the Tampa Bay Buccaneers in the regular season is 11-6, for a winning percentage of .647.

The wind chill for the Giants' game against the Green Bay Packers in the 2007 NFC Championship Game on Jan. 20, 2008, was minus 23 degrees. The regular temperature was minus 1 degree. This was the coldest game in Giants history. Lawrence Tyne sealed the game with a 47-yard field goal in overtime. It was the first time in Lambeau Field history that an opponent kicked a field goal of more than 40 yards in a postseason game. New York won 23-20.

By The Numbers

•••ooo

New York Giants

48

F
O
O
T
B
A
L
L

Len Younce punted 48 times in 1944, most in the NFL that season. He was the first Giants player to lead the league in this category.

Joe Montgomery led the Giants with 348 rushing yards in 1999. He is the last player to lead the team with fewer than 500 total rushing yards for the season.

Emlen Tunnell signed with the Giants in 1948, the first black player to sign with New York.

The Rams gained 448 yards against the Giants in the 1989 NFC Divisional Playoffs. This is the most yards the Giants allowed in a postseason game since 1958.

Kyle Rote recorded 48 career receiving touchdowns from 1951-61. This would stand as the Giants career record until broken by Amani Toomer in 2007.

The Giants attempted just 148 passes in 1942, led by Tuffy Leemans 42 attempts. The team total is the second fewest attempts in team history behind the 125 attempts in 1944.

Featured Figure

The first regular-season game in Giants Stadium took place on Sunday, Oct. 10, 1976. The Giants lost the inaugural game in their new home 14-24 to the Dallas Cowboys. The last game in the stadium was on Jan. 3, 2010. New York also lost that game, 7-44 to the Minnesota Vikings.

By The Numbers

• • • ○ ○ ○

New York Giants

ooo••• ——————————————— 49

F
O
O
T
B
A
L
L

Tiki Barber rushed for 10,449 yards as a Giant from 1997-2006, the franchise record for career rushing yards. He gained more than 1,500 rushing yards in each of his last three seasons.

New York finished 6-6 in 1949. It was the team's third straight non-winning season, the longest streak in franchise history up to that point.

New York's all-time record against the Green Bay Packers in the regular season is 21-26-2, for a winning percentage of .449.

The Giants lost 7-56 at home to the Chicago Bears on Nov. 14, 1943. The 49-point differential represents the largest home loss in Giants history.

Homer Jones had four receptions for 196 yards against the Washington Redskins on Oct. 1, 1967. His 49.0-yard average per reception ranks second of all time in Giants history.

Featured Figure

Ray Handley coached the Giants for two seasons after Bill Parcells' retirement in 1990. He led the team to a 14-18 record for a .428 winning percentage.New York has played five teams 50 or more times: the Arizona Cardinals (79-42-2), Dallas Cowboys (39-56-2), Philadelphia Eagles (79-71-2), Pittsburgh Steelers (44-28-3) and Washington Redskins (91-61-4).

By The Numbers

•••ooo

New York Giants

ooo ...

F
O
O
T
B
A
L
L

In 1950 the NFL expanded and renamed the Eastern and Western Divisions the American and National Conference, renaming them again in 1953 to the Eastern and Western Conference. The Giants were placed in the American Division with the Cleveland Browns, Pittsburgh Steelers, Philadelphia Eagles, Chicago Cardinals and Washington Redskins. NY finished the regular season 10-2, the team's first winning season since 1946. They faced the Browns in the Divisional Playoff Game. The two teams combined for three field goals and one safety, but the Giants lost 3-8. It was the team's sixth consecutive loss in the playoffs.

New York had an all-time record of 2-2 at home in playoff games at Yankee Stadium for a winning percentage of .500.

New York finished the 1950s with a record of 76-41-3 for a .646 winning percentage.

NY has an all-time regular-season winning percentage of .500 against the Atlanta Falcons (10-10) and Carolina Panthers (3-3).

NY retired Ken Strong's jersey #50 in 1947. He played fullback and kicker for nine seasons during the 1930s and 1940s.

By The Numbers

... ooo

New York Giants

○ ○ ○ • • •

51

F O O T B A L L

The New York Giants chose Southern Methodist running back Kyle Rote with the NFL's bonus pick in the 1951 NFL Draft. The bonus choice was essentially the No. 1 overall draft pick and was used by the NFL from 1947-58. Rote played 11 seasons with the Giants, and was a four-time Pro Bowler (1953-56).

Steve Owen led the Giants to 151 wins during his tenure as the team's head coach from 1931-53. His overall regular season record was 151-100-17 for a .602 winning percentage. He led the Giants to two NFL Championships and had only six losing seasons in 23 years. Owen was inducted into the Pro Football Hall of Fame in 1966.

In 1963 Giants cornerback Dick Lynch led the NFL with nine interceptions, 251 interception return yards and three interceptions returned for touchdown. His 251 interception return yards matched the team season record set by Emlen Tunnell in 1949. Lynch's three interceptions for touchdowns is also a team record.

Plaxico Burress caught 11 passes for 151 yards in the 2007 NFC Championship Game. His longest reception for the game went for 32 yards. He is one of three Giants to gain more than 150 receiving yards in a postseason game.

Featured Figure

Homer Jones gained 1,209 receiving yards in 1967. This would stand as the Giants single-season record until 2002.

• • • ○ ○ ○

By The Numbers

New York Giants

○ ○ ○ ● ● ●

52

F O O T B A L L

Ward Cuff led the NFL with 152 interception return yards in 1941, the first Giant to lead the league in this category. The last Giant to lead this category for a season was Dick Lynch in 1963.

Don Chandler made 52 PATs in 1963, breaking the record of 47 PATs made in a season that he set the previous year, which broke the record of 46 that was set by Pat Summerall in 1961.

New York has played on Monday Night Football a total of 52 times. The team's overall record is 21-31-1, for a .413 winning percentage, with a home record of 6-8 and away record of 15-23-1. The last season the team did not play on Monday Night was in 2004.

Phil Simms averaged 252.8 yards passing per game in 1984. This ranks second on the Giants all-time list for the category.

Jim Patton recorded 52 interceptions during his career with the Giants from 1955-66. This ranks second of all time in team history.

The Giants made a team record 52 PATs in 1963.

Hakeem Nicks led the Giants with 1,052 receiving yards in 2010.

By The Numbers

● ● ● ○ ○ ○

New York Giants

○ ○ ○ • • •

53

**F
O
O
T
B
A
L
L**

Giants owner Tim Mara turned over a check for $115,153 to the New York City Unemployment Fund in 1930 to help families during the Great Depression. The money was raised from a charity game between the Giants and a Notre Dame All-Star team made up of past and present players. The game was played at the Polo Grounds on Dec. 14, and many of the 50,000 plus fans cheered on for the Fighting Irish. Up 15-0 at halftime, New York played most of the second string in the second half. Even that was too much for Notre Dame. New York won 22-0. The check totaled the entire amount of receipts for the game. Mara lost money after paying for Notre Dame's expenses, but the game did help stamp out questions about whether or not an NFL team could beat a top-notch college team.

Tiki Barber fumbled the football 53 times during his Giants career. He ranks fourth on the team's career list, but has the most among non-quarterbacks.

NY beat the Redskins 53-0 on Nov. 5, 1961. This is the Giants' largest victory over the Redskins.

Joe Morris gained 553 career rushing yards in the postseason, a Giants career record.

Steve Owen retired as head coach following New York's 3-9 finish in 1953.

Phil McConkey returned 53 punts in 1985, a Giants single-season record.

By The Numbers

• • • ○ ○ ○

New York Giants

54

F O O T B A L L

New York finished 7-5 in 1954 despite a stingy defense that ranked No. 1 in the league in interceptions, fumbles and turnovers. The defense also ranked second in touchdowns allowed and third in rushing yards and passing yards allowed. However, the offense ranked ninth in touchdowns scored.

The Giants hired future Pro Football Hall of Fame coaches Vince Lombardi and Tom Landry in 1954. Lombardi served as offensive coordinator though 1958 and Landry served as defensive coordinator through 1959. The team won one NFL Championship, and played in another, while both of these legendary coaches were in New York.

The NY defense led the league with 54 sacks in 1998. Michael Strahan led the team with 15.0 sacks.

Kerry Collins averaged 254.6 passing yards per game in 2002. This is a NY single-season record.

Amani Toomer had a team record 54 career receiving touchdowns in his Giants career.

The Giants defense allowed 63 points to the Steelers in 1954, tied for second as the single-game record for points allowed.

Featured Figure

NY has an all-time regular-season record of 16-16 against current AFC South teams for a winning percentage of .500.

By The Numbers

New York Giants

○ ○ ○ • • • ————————————————— ⊕ **55**

F
O
O
Eli Manning completed 19 of 34 passes for 255 yards in Super Bowl XLII, a team record for most passing yards in a Super Bowl. Manning also threw two touchdowns and one interception and finished the game with a quarterback rating of 87.3.

T
B
The Giants have an all-time record of 20-24 in the postseason for a winning percentage of .455.

A
L
L
Phil Simms lost 434 yards due to sacks in 1984, leading the NFL in this category for the season. He was sacked 55 times, which is a Giants single-season record. He was also sacked 53 times in 1988 and 52 times in 1985. Simms is the only Giants quarterback to have been sacked 50 or more times in a season.

A preseason game between the Giants and Los Angeles Rams went into sudden death overtime in 1955. This was the first preseason game to be played under these rules. New York lost the game 17-23.

The Giants allowed just 55 first downs on the ground in 1982. This broke the team record low of 58 that was set in 1938.

Brian Mitchell returned 55 kickoffs for the Giants in 2003. This broke the team's single-season record of 43 that was set by David Patten in 1998.

By The Numbers

• • • ○ ○ ○

New York Giants

○○○ • • • ————————————————— **56**

F
O
O
T
B
A
L
L

New York beat the Philadelphia Eagles 56-0 on Oct. 15, 1933, the first-ever meeting between the two teams. The point differential is a Giants record for largest margin of victory.

Don Chandler attempted 56 PATs in 1963, breaking the record of 48 PATs attempts in a season that he set the previous year. That record broke the record of 46 that was set by Pat Summerall in 1961.

Ali Haji-Sheikh successfully made two 56-yard field goals in 1983. He holds NY's record for the longest made field goal.

New York finished the regular season 8-3-1 in 1956, first place in the division. They played the Chicago Bears in the NFL Championship Game. It was the Giants' first appearance in the title game since 1946. The Giants opened up a 34-7 lead by halftime and won the game 47-7, the team's first NFL title since 1938. New York players brought home a lot of hardware that season. Linebacker Sam Huff was named NFL Rookie of the Year, Rosie Brown was named NFL Lineman of the Year and Frank Gifford was named NFL Player of the Year.

The Giants began playing home games at Yankee Stadium in 1956.

New York retired Lawrence Taylor's jersey #56 at halftime of a Monday Night Football Game against the Minnesota Vikings on Oct. 10, 1994.

By The Numbers

• • • ○○○

New York Giants

○ ○ ○ • • •

F
O
O
T
B
A
L
L

Domenik Hixon returned 57 kickoffs in 2009, a Giants single-season record.

The Giants lost the last three games in 1957, finishing second in the division. Two of the losses came to the Cleveland Browns, winners of the division. Frank Gifford ranked in the top ten of the league in rushing and receiving for the second consecutive year.

Homer Jones gained 1,057 yards receiving with the Giants in 1968, his third consecutive season with 1,000 receiving yards. He was the second player in franchise history to accomplish this feat. Jones also led the league in receiving touchdowns (13) and total touchdowns (14) in 1968.

Tiki Barber carried the ball 357 times in 2005, a Giants single-season record for attempts. He had 30 or more attempts in a game twice that season and his lowest single game total was 13 attempts in Week 1.

In 1935 Giants quarterback Ed Danowski led the NFL with 57 pass completions and attempts with 113. His completion total set a team single-season record.

Eli Manning had 557 pass attempts in 2005. This is a Giants record for the most attempts in a single season.

Phil Simms threw 157 interceptions during his NFL career. He ranks second on the Giants' all-time list for the category.

By The Numbers

• • • ○ ○ ○

New York Giants

○ ○ ○ ● ● ●

F
O
O
T
B
A
L
L

The 1958 NFL Championship Game is often referred to as "The Greatest Game Ever Played." The game between the New York Giants and Baltimore Colts was held at the old Yankee Stadium on Dec. 28. Both teams entered the game with regular-season records of 9-3. NBC televised the game nationally. Baltimore scored two touchdowns following turnovers by New York and led the Giants 14-3 at halftime. In the third quarter, the Colts turned the ball over on downs from the Giants' 5-yard line. New York subsequently went 95 yards to score and cut the Colts' lead to four. The Giants took a 17-14 lead early in the fourth quarter, but Johnny Unitas led the Colts down the field for the tying field goal with 20 seconds left in regulation. But prior to the game, the sudden-death overtime rule was implemented by the commissioner of the NFL. The Giants won the coin toss but went three-and-out. Unitas led his team 80 yards for the winning score. This game is credited with increasing national interest in professional football and it included 17 future members of the Pro Football Hall of Fame.

In a game against the Chicago Bears on Nov. 27, 1927, Giants punter Hinkey Haines completed a 58-yard pass to Charlie Corgan on a fake punt from New York's own end zone. The drive ended in the go-ahead score and the Giants won 13-7. Even though there were two games left in the season, this win secured New York's first NFL Championship, which at the time was decided based on the best record.

By The Numbers

In 1983 the Giants led the NFL in turnovers with 58.

● ● ● ○ ○ ○

New York Giants

ooo•••

F
O
O
T
B
A
L
L

Joe Morris ran the ball 24 times for 159 yards in the Giants win against the 49ers in the 1986 NFC Championship Game.

Giants co-founder Tim Mara died on Feb. 17, 1959.

The Giants finished the 1959 regular season with a record of 10-2, the team's best record since 1950. New York faced the Baltimore Colts in the 1959 NFL Championship Game, a rematch of the previous year. The Giants were unable to finish drives in the first three quarters, but led 9-7 after three Pat Summerall field goals. Baltimore then scored 24-unanswered points and took a commanding 31-9 lead. Giants receiver Bob Schnelker caught a 32-yard touchdown pass from Charlie Conerly in the fourth quarter. New York lost the game 16-31.

Giants tight end Bob Tucker led the NFL with 59 receptions in 1971. He is the first New York tight end to lead the league in receptions.

Willie Ponder gained 259 kickoff return yards against the Steelers in 2004, a team single-game record. He broke the record of 207 yards set by Joe Scott against the Rams in 1948.

New York has an all-time regular-season record of 38-30 against current teams in the NFC South for a winning percentage of .559.

By The Numbers

•••ooo

New York Giants

○ ○ ○ • • •

F
O
O
T
B
A
L
L

New York's team song, "Fight, You Fightin' Giants," was written in 1960 by Herb Steiner, Cy Gillis and Kyle Rote.

New York has an all-time winning percentage in the regular season of .600 against the Jacksonville Jaguars (3-2), Seattle Seahawks (9-6) and New England Patriots (3-5).

Each of the four HD video display boards located in the corners at MetLife Stadium is 30 x 118 feet, for a grand total of 14,160 square feet of viewing area.

Osi Umenyiora has recorded 60 sacks during his 8-year career with the Giants. He currently ranks 90th on the NFL's all-time sack list.

Joe Danelo attempted 160 career field goals as a Giant. He is third on the all-time list.

Tiki Barber rushed for 1,860 yards in 2005, a NY single-season record.

New York finished the 1960s with a regular-season record of 69-63-6 for a .522 winning percentage.

NY's all-time record against the New Orleans Saints in the regular season is 14-11 (.560).

The Giants allowed the Colts to gain 460 yards in the 1958 NFL Championship Game, a team record for yards allowed in the postseason.

By The Numbers

• • • ○ ○ ○

New York Giants

○ ○ ○ • • •

F
O
O
T
B
A
L
L

Emlen Tunnell returned 261 punts in his Giants career, a team record.

Pete Gogolak scored in 61 consecutive games from 1969-73, a Giants record.

In 1961 the Giants traded offensive lineman Lou Cordileone to the San Francisco 49ers for quarterback Y.A. Tittle. He led the team to a 10-3-1 regular-season record under new Giants head coach Allie Sherman.

New York faced off against the Green Bay Packers in the 1961 NFL Championship Game. For the regular season, the Giants defense ranked No. 1 in fewest points allowed and the Packers offense ranked No. 1 in most points scored. The 20-degree weather made field conditions questionable and while the Packers chose to wear cleats, the Giants chose sneakers, expecting better grip on a frozen field. After a scoreless first quarter, Green Bay rattled off 37-unanswered points and shut out the Giants 37-0. The game was played at what would become Lambeau Field. This was the first championship for Packer head coach, and former Giants assistant, Vince Lombardi.

The Giants added the NY logo to the helmet in 1961.

Rodney Hampton rushed for 161 yards against the Minnesota Vikings in the 1993 Wild Card Playoffs, tying a Giants postseason record initially set by Rob Carpenter against Philadelphia in the 1981 Wild Card Playoffs.

By The Numbers

• • • ○ ○ ○

New York Giants

○○○•••————————————————— 62

F
O
O
T
B
A
L
L

Phil Simms passed for 33,462 yards from 1979-93. This is the Giants' career passing record. He passed for 2,000 or more yards for 10 of his 14 seasons in New York.

Giants quarterback Charlie Conerly punted for 5,062 yards during his 14-year career with the team.

The Giants scored 62 points against the Philadelphia Eagles on Nov. 26, 1972. This is a team record for most points scored in a game.

New York had a regular-season record of 63-48-5 at Yankee Stadium for a winning percentage of .562.

The Giants won the last nine games of the 1962 season to finish 12-2 and claim the Eastern Conference crown. They faced the Green Bay Packers in the NFL Championship for the second consecutive year. The Packers jumped out to a 10-0 lead before Giants defensive back Erich Barnes blocked a Green Bay punt that was recovered in the end zone by defensive end Jim Collier for New York's only points of the game. Despite outgaining the Packers 291-244 yards, New York lost 7-16, an unfortunate day for the 64,892 fans that passed through the turnstiles at Yankee Stadium to watch the game. This was the last Giants playoff game at Yankee Stadium.

Giants defensive end Andy Robustelli received the Bert Bell Award as the NFL's Most Outstanding Player in 1962.

By The Numbers

•••○○○

New York Giants

63

F O O T B A L L

Jim Lee Howell had a regular-season winning percentage of .663 as Giants head coach from 1954-60. This is the highest among all New York head coaches. He led the team to a record of 53-27-4 during those seven seasons.

NFL Hall of Fame head coach Tom Landry was a defensive back for the Giants from 1950-55 and an assistant coach from 1954-59 before becoming head coach of the Dallas Cowboys in 1960. Landry punted for a total of 3,363 yards in 1952, the most of any Giant that punted in 12 or fewer games in a season. He also holds the team record for the most consecutive games with an interception, with seven.

The Giants finished 11-3 in 1963, winning their third consecutive Eastern Division Title. The offense averaged 32 points a game behind Y.A. Tittle's NFL record-setting 36 passing touchdowns, since broken. New York faced the Chicago Bears in the NFL Championship Game. It was the first time since the Giants won the 1956 NFL Championship that the two teams met in the playoffs. Tittle led the Giants to a first quarter touchdown to give NY a 7-0 lead but injured his knee later in the quarter. Playing injured most of the game, Tittle was unable to move the ball against the Chicago defense, nicknamed the "Monsters of the Midway." He threw five interceptions for the game after throwing just 14 interceptions during the regular season. New York lost 10-14 and wouldn't make the playoffs again for 22 years.

By The Numbers

• • • ○ ○ ○

New York Giants

F
O
O
T
B
A
L
L

Phil Simms played in 164 games as a Giant, the most games played of any Giants quarterback. Simms started in 16 regular-season games four different years.

Giants running back Ken Strong led the NFL in scoring in 1933 with 64 points. For the season, Strong had three rushing touchdowns, two receiving touchdowns one interception returned for touchdown, five field goals made and 13 extra-points made.

For the first time in 17 years, the Giants finished last in the Eastern Conference in 1964. The season record of 2-10-2 was the fewest wins since 1947 and worst winning percentage in franchise history. Frank Gifford and Alex Webster announced their retirements following the end of the season. These two players accounted for a combined 16,360 yards from scrimmage during their careers in New York.

New York's all-time record against the Oakland Raiders in the regular season is 4-7, for a winning percentage of .364.

Featured Figure

Tuffy Leemans led the Giants in rushing five seasons (1936, 1938-41), receiving two seasons (1937, 1939) and passing two seasons (1941-42). He is the only New York player to have led each of these categories at least once during his career.

By The Numbers

New York Giants

○ ○ ○ • • • ——————————— **65**

F
O
O
T
B
A
L
L

The New York Giants chose Auburn fullback Tucker Frederickson with the No. 1 overall draft pick in the 1965 NFL Draft. Frederickson played six seasons with the Giants and made the Pro Bowl his rookie season. He ranks 16th on New York's career rushing yards list with 2,209 yards.

Lindon Crow led the NFL in fumble return yards in 1960 with 65 yards, the first Giants player to lead the league in this category.

Y.A. Tittle announced his retirement from football on Jan. 22, 1965.

Team President Jack Mara, son of co-founder Tim Mara, died on June 15, 1965.

The Giants finished 7-7 in 1965, tied for second place in the Eastern Division.

The Detroit Lions ran the ball 65 times for 246 yards against the Giants in the 1935 NFL Championship Game, setting NY records for opponent rushing attempts and rushing yards in a postseason game.

New York's all-time record against the Arizona Cardinals in the regular season is 79-42-2, for a winning percentage of .650.

By The Numbers

• • • ○ ○ ○

New York Giants

○ ○ ○ • • • ———————————————

66

F
O
O
T
B
A
L
L

Official seating capacity at MetLife Stadium is 82,566, the highest among all NFL stadiums.

Giants defensive end Neal Adams returned an interception 66 yards for a touchdown in 1942, good enough to be the longest return that season in the NFL.

Brad Maynard punted for 4,566 yards in 1998, a Giants single-season record. This total places him 11th of all time on the NFL's list for this category. Maynard punted for 4,531 yards in 1997, second on the Giants' single-season list. He is the only Giants player to surpass the 4,500 punt yardage mark in a season.

The Giants finished with a 1-12-1 record in 1966, a franchise record for the fewest wins in a season and the team's worst-ever winning percentage at .107. The defense allowed a then record 501 points during the season, 35.8 points per game.

In 1966, Giants kicker Pete Gogolak became the first player from the American Football League to play in the NFL. New York signed him away from the Buffalo Bills, ending a former "gentleman's agreement" between the league owners. Afterwards, it became common for teams from both leagues to sign players from the other league prior to merging in 1970.

Eli Manning has been sacked 166 times in his career with the Giants.

By The Numbers

• • • ○ ○ ○

New York Giants

ooo•••

F
O
O
T
B
A
L
L

Charlie Conerly threw 167 interceptions as a Giants quarterback, a team record for the most in a career. He led the NFL in 1953 with 25 interceptions, and threw 20 or more interceptions two other seasons during his career.

Michael Strahan recorded 667 tackles during his Giants career, a team record for career tackles. Tackles did not become an official NFL statistic until 2001.

Y.A. Tittle threw 367 passes in 1963 and completed 36 for touchdowns. His .981 touchdowns per attempt percentage is a franchise high among quarterbacks with 100 or more attempts in a season.

In 1990 Dave Meggett led the NFL with 467 punt return yards, the last Giant to lead the league in this category.

New York had a regular-season record of 130-62-11 at the Polo Grounds for a winning percentage of .667.

Willie Ponder gained 967 yards on kickoff returns in 2004 and 904 yards in 2005. He is the only Giants player to have surpassed 900 kickoff return yards in a season twice.

Kerry Collins attempted 568 passes in 2001, a Giants single-season record. He completed 327 of the passes for 3,764 yards.

NY's all-time record against the Houston Texans in the regular season is 2-1, for a winning percentage of .667.

By The Numbers

•••ooo

New York Giants

○ ○ ○ • • • ─────────────────────────── 68

F
O
O
T
B
A
L
L

Pete Gogolak made 268 PATs in his Giants career, a team record.

Head coach Allie Sherman led the team to a 7-7 record in 1968, his fifth consecutive non-winning season and his last season at the helm.

Del Shofner caught 68 passes in 1961. His single-season reception total would stand as the Giants' record for 22 years until broken by Earnest Gray's 78 receptions in 1983.

Jason Sehorn gained 68 yards on interceptions in the postseason during his career in New York. Sehorn only returned two of his four postseason interceptions, one for 36 yards and the other for 38. He is the only Giants players with more than 50 interception yards in the postseason.

Amani Toomer recorded 668 receptions in his career with the Giants. This is a team career record.

Featured Figure

The first time a logo appeared on the side of the Giants' helmets was in 1961 when a lowercase "ny" logo was added. This was replaced by an italic uppercase "NY" logo in 1975, which lasted only one season before being replaced by the "Giants" logo. The original lowercase "ny" returned to the helmet in 1994 and remains an integral part of the helmet.

By The Numbers

• • • ○ ○ ○

New York Giants

○ ○ ○ • • •

F
O
O
T
B
A
L
L

Del Shofner gained 269 receiving yards against the Washington Redskins on Oct. 28, 1962, a Giants single-game record. Even though the Giants won the game 49-34, Shofner scored just once. He ranks 10th on the Giants' career receiving list with 4,315 yards. His 18.1 yards-per-reception average ranks him third on the Giants' all-time list among receivers with 100 or more career receptions.

Because of dual occupancy between the Giants and Jets, Giants Stadium hosted 469 regular-season NFL games, more than any other stadium. The Jets began playing home games at Giants Stadium in 1984.

Fran Tarkenton started 69 games as a Giants quarterback from 1967-71. Minnesota traded him to New York in 1967 and the Giants returned the favor following the 1971 season. He had a 33-36 record with the Giants.

As a team, the Giants rushed for just 769 yards in 1945. This is a franchise season low. The only other time the team failed to surpass the 1,000-yard mark in a season was its 842-yard total in 1982, which was shortened due to strike.

Former Giants running back Alex Webster was announced as the team's head coach prior to the 1969 season.

The Giants and Jets met for the first time in the preseason in 1969, the Giants lost 14-37.

By The Numbers

• • • ○ ○ ○

New York Giants

○○○ ••• ———————————————————

F
O
O
T
B
A
L
L

Joe Danelo made 170 PATs during his Giants career, nearly 100 behind franchise leading Pete Gogolak's total.

New York had an all-time record of 7-3 at home in playoff games in Giants Stadium for a winning percentage of .700.

New York finished the 1970s with a regular-season record of 50-93-1 for a .350 winning percentage. This is NY's lowest winning percentage over a decade time frame and the only losing decade in team history. The Giants did not play in a single postseason game during the decade.

Mel Hein played 170 games with the Giants from 1931-45, a career service record that would not be broken until 1972. He never missed an NFL game and failed to play every snap just twice.

In 1938 Giants quarterback Ed Danowski led the NFL with 70 pass completions. This would stand as NY's single-season record until 1946.

Fran Tarkenton led the Giants to five game-winning drives in 1970. Kerry Collins matched this record in 2002 and Eli Manning surpassed it with six in 2007.

Kerry Collins had 70 passes intercepted in his career with the Giants, fifth most in team history.

By The Numbers

••• ○○○

New York Giants

F
O
O
T
B
A
L
L

Kerry Collins played in 71 games as a Giants quarterback from 1999-2003. He averaged 237.7 passing yards per game, a Giants career record.

New York finished 4-10 in 1971. Fran Tarkenton, who passed for just 11 touchdowns, a career low at that point, asked to be traded back to the Vikings. He later led the Vikings to three Super Bowl appearances, all losses.

The Giants finished with a 9-2-1 record in 1951, with both loses to the Cleveland Browns. New York running back Eddie Price led the NFL that season with 971 rushing yards.

New York has an all-time regular-season record of 115-86-2 against current teams in the NFC West for a winning percentage of .571.

Jeremy Shockey had 371 career receptions during his time with the Giants. This is a team career record among tight ends.

Featured Figure

Only three Giants players have led the NFL in average yards per rushing attempt in a season, and each of them led the league twice: Tuffy Leemans, 69.2 yards in 1936 and 47.4 yards in 1940; Bill Paschal, 63.6 yards in 1943, and 73.7 yards in 1944; and Eddie Price, 70.3 yards in 1950 and 80.9 yards in.

By The Numbers

New York Giants

ooo•••

72

**F
O
O
T
B
A
L
L**

U2 held a concert in front of 84,472 fans at Giants Stadium on Sept. 24, 2009, a record crowd for any event held at the venue. This broke the previous record set when Pope John Paul II celebrated Mass at the stadium in 1995.

The Giants finished 8-6 in 1972, the second winning season under head coach Alex Webster.

In 1972 Ron Johnson became the first Giants player to rush for 1,000 yards. He gained 1,182 yards on 298 attempts.

Norm Snead led the NFL in 1972 with a pass completion percentage of .603. He and Y.A. Tittle are the only Giants players to have led the league in this category. Tittle led the NFL with a .602 completion percentage in 1963.

The Giants tied a team single-game record against the Eagles in 1972 with eight touchdowns scored. NY also scored eight touchdowns against the Eagles in 1933 and against the Colts in 1950.

The Giants defense gave up 72 points to the Washington Redskins on Nov. 27, 1966. This is the team record for the most points allowed in a game.

Scott Brunner completed a 72-yard pass to Earnest Gray against the 49ers in the 1981 Wild Card Playoffs. This is the longest passing play in Giants postseason history.

By The Numbers

•••ooo

New York Giants

○ ○ ○ • • •

F
O
O
T
B
A
L
L

Kerry Collins passed for 4,073 yards in 2002, a Giants single-season record. He completed 335 of 545 passes and recorded 19 passing touchdowns.

New York head coach Alex Webster announced his retirement prior to the last game in 1973. The Giants were no match for the Fran Tarkenton-led Vikings, losing the last game 7-31 and finishing the season 2-11-1.

The Giants played the first two games of the 1973 season at Yankee Stadium and the remaining home games at the Yale Bowl in New Haven, Conn.

Kerry Collins completed 1,447 of 2,473 pass attempts during his Giants career. His .585 career completion percentage is the highest among players with 1,000 or more attempts.

Harry Newman led the NFL with 973 passing yards in 1933. This total would stand as the Giants' single-season record until 1946.

Charlie Conerly threw for 173 touchdowns during his Giants career. He currently ranks second on the team's all-time list for the category, just six ahead of Eli Manning as of the end of the 2010 season.

Featured Figure

New York's all-time record against the Miami Dolphins in the regular season is 4-2, for a winning percentage of .667.

By The Numbers

• • • ○ ○ ○

New York Giants

○ ○ ○ ● ● ● ─────────────── 74

F
O
O
T
B
A
L
L

Defensive back Emlen Tunnell recorded 74 interceptions during his career with the Giants, a team career record. He ranks second on the NFL career interception list with 79.

Bill Arnsparger became New York's ninth head coach prior to the 1974 season. Different coach, same results, as the Giants finished with just two wins for the second consecutive year.

Len Younce recorded a 74-yard punt against the Chicago Bears in 1943. This was matched by Don Chandler in 1964 and would stand as the Giants single-game record until broken by Rodney Williams' 90-yard punt against Denver in 2001.

Terry Kinard gained 574 yards off interceptions during his career with the Giants. He ranks third of all time in Giants history. However, his 21.3 yard average per interception ranks No. 1 among the top 10 interceptors in Giants history.

Jeremy Shockey had 74 receptions in 2002. This is a Giants single-season record for the most receptions by a tight end.

Featured Figure

Steve Owen coached his last game with the Giants against the Detroit Lions on Dec. 13, 1953. His 23-year tenure was closed out with a 3-9 home loss.

By The Numbers

● ● ● ○ ○ ○

74

New York Giants

○ ○ ○ ● ● ●

(75)

F
O
O
T
B
A
L
L

Tom Landry punted 75 times for the Giants in 1955, the most in the NFL that season.

New York had a regular-season record of 158-117 at Giants Stadium for a winning percentage of .575.

The Giants played all of their home games at Shea Stadium in 1975.

Bob Schnelker caught nine passes for 175 yards and one touchdown against the Baltimore Colts in the 1959 NFL Championship Game. Schnelker's total receiving yards gained is a Giants postseason record. His longest reception on the day went for 48 yards.

New York's all-time record against the Cincinnati Bengals in the regular season is 3-5, for a winning percentage of .375.

Kerry Collins passed for 16,875 yards with the Giants. He ranks fourth of all time for the category.

Carl Lockhart returned 41 career interceptions 475 yards for the Giants from 1965-75.

Featured Figure

Charlie Conerly led the NFL in 1956 and 1959 with the lowest percentage of pass attempts intercepted. He is the only Giants player to have led the league in this category more than once.

By The Numbers

● ● ● ○ ○ ○

New York Giants

76

F O O T B A L L

Phil Simms completed 2,576 passes as a Giants quarterback, a team career record. He completed 200 or more passes in a season six times.

Joe Danelo attempted 176 PATs during his 13 seasons with the Giants (1976-82). He ranks second on the team's all-time list for the category.

The Giants moved into Giants Stadium in 1976.

In 1976, Bill Arnsparger was fired mid-season as New York's head coach after the team started 0-7. He led the Giants to a record of 7-28 during his tenure as head coach. New York promoted assistant coach John McVay to head coach after Arnsparger's release. The team finished the season 3-4 under McVay.

Future Hall of Famer, and former Miami Dolphins great, Larry Csonka signed with the Giants in 1976. He led the team in touchdowns that season with four.

The Giants lost the first nine games of the 1976 season. This is the most consecutive losses in team history. New York ended the season with a record of 3-11.

Jeff Hostetler threw 76 passes in the postseason with the Giants without throwing a single interception. This is the lowest pass interception percentage in team history among players with 50 or more attempts.

By The Numbers

New York Giants

○ ○ ○ ● ● ● ─────────────────────────── ⊕ 77

F
O
O
Phil Simms was sacked a team-record 477 times during his career with the Giants. He was sacked an average of two or more times per game in 13 of his 15 seasons with the Giants and a career average of 2.9 times per game.

T
B
Pete Gogolak attempted 277 PATs during his Giants career, a team single-season record.

A
L
L
Bill Parcells led the Giants to 77 wins during his tenure as head coach. He ranks second on the all-time list in franchise history. His overall record in NY was 77-49-1, and his winning percentage of .611 ranks second of all time in franchise history among coaches that lasted three or more seasons.

Bob Hammond led the Giants with 577 rushing yards in 1977.

New York scored just 17 offensive touchdowns in 1977 and finished the season with a 5-9 record.

Morris "Red" Badgro played six seasons with the Giants and was named All-NFL three times. He was inducted into the Pro Football Hall of Fame in 1981 at the age of 77.

Eli Manning has lost 1,177 yards due to sacks during his Giants career.

Bill Paschal scored on a 77-yard rushing attempt in 1945. This was the longest in the NFL that season.

By The Numbers

● ● ● ○ ○ ○

New York Giants

○ ○ ○ ● ● ● ────────────────────

F
O
Jeff Feagles recorded 178 punts inside the 20-yard line from 2003-09, a Giants career record for the most punts downed inside the 20.

O
T
B
New York started the 1978 season 5-3 but finished the second half 1-7. Jim McVay was released as head coach after leading the Giants to a 15-23 career record.

A
L
L
Philadelphia Eagles defensive back Herman Edwards returned a fumble 26 yards for the Eagles' go-ahead score in the waning seconds on Nov. 19, 1978. Later known simply as "The Fumble" to Giants fans, the play is considered one of the worst decisions in NFL history and led to a mindset change throughout the league. With possession, and the Eagles without timeouts, the Giants only had to take a knee to seal a 17-12 victory. Instead, an attempt by New York quarterback Joe Pisarcik to hand the ball off to Larry Csonka resulted in the fumble. Prior to this game, many players and coaches in the NFL considered kneeling less than honorable. After the shocking result, the Giants wasted no time instituting the "Victory Formation." They used the new formation before halftime the following week to maintain a 10-7 lead against the Buffalo Bills, but eventually lost the game after being outscored 7-34 in the second half.

Tiki Barber scored on a 78-yard run against the Arizona Cardinals on Sept. 3, 2000. This is the longest rushing play to result in a touchdown in a Giants home game.

By The Numbers

────────── ● ● ● ○ ○ ○

New York Giants

○ ○ ○ • • •

F
O
O
T
B
A
L
L

New York has an all-time record of 11-8 at home in playoff games for a .579 winning percentage.

The Giants drafted Phil Simms out of Morehead St. with the seventh pick overall of the 1979 NFL Draft. Simms started 11 games his rookie season and had 13 touchdown passes, the most for a New York quarterback since Norm Snead's 17 in 1972.

Amani Toomer had 79 receptions in 1999, breaking the previous Giants single-season record of 78 set by Earnest Gray in 1983.

In 1979, Giants punter Dave Jennings led the NFC with an average of 42.7 yards per punt.

Frank Gifford's longest rushing play in his Giants career was 79 yards, which he gained against the Redskins in 1959.

Joe Scott gained 279 all-purpose yards against the Rams on Nov. 14, 1948. This is a Giants team record for the most all-purpose yards in a game.

Featured Figure

Tiki Barber gained 2,000 or more combined net yards four different times. He had 2,085 combined net yards in 2000; 2,096 in 2004; 2,390 in 2005; and 2,127 in 2006. Barber is the only Giant to surpass the 2,000 combined net yards mark in a season.

By The Numbers

• • • ○ ○ ○

New York Giants

○○○ ••• ———————————————— 80

F
O
O
T
B
A
L
L

New York started the 1980 season 1-8, being outscored 76-229 in the seven losses. However, the Giants had a slight turnaround and won three of the remaining seven games. Phil Simms passed for over 2,000 yards but the young quarterback still threw four more interceptions than touchdowns for the season. Billy Taylor led the team with 580 rushing yards.

In 1980, Giants punter Dave Jennings led the NFL with an average of 44.8 yards per punt.

New York finished the 1980s with a regular-season record of 81-70-1 for a .536 winning percentage.

New York's stifling defense in the 1980s was commonly referred to as the "Big Blue Wrecking Crew."

The Giants passed for a team postseason record 380 yards against the Minnesota Vikings in the 2000 NFC Championship Game.

NY returned 80 kickoffs in 1966, a team single-season record for the most kickoffs returned.

Brandon Jacobs has gained 4,880 yards from scrimmage during his career with the Giants. He has gained 4,278 yards rushing and 602 yards receiving.

The Giants ran the ball 580 times in 1978. This stood as the NY record until 1985 when the team had 581 attempts.

By The Numbers

••• ○○○

New York Giants

F O O T B A L L

Andy Headen led the NFL in fumble return yards in 1984 with 81 yards. He is the last Giants player to lead the league in this category.

Lawrence Taylor was named Defensive Rookie of the Year by the Associated Press in 1981. He is the only Giants player to receive this recognition.

Del Shofner gained 1,181 receiving yards in 1963, his third consecutive season with 1,000 receiving yards. He is the first player in franchise history to surpass the 1,000 receiving-yard mark three consecutive years; however, he failed to gain more than 400 yards in any of his remaining four seasons with the team.

The Giants finished 9-7 in 1981, the team's first winning season since 1972.

The Giants faced the 49ers in the 1981 NFC Divisional Playoffs. New York stayed close to San Francisco, the team with the best record in the league that season. But the 49ers pulled away in the fourth quarter and NY lost 24-38.

In 1981 Joe Danelo led the NFL in field goal attempts with 38. He is the only Giants player to have led the league in this category.

Featured Figure

The Giants have an all-time postseason record of 3-15 on the road for a .200 winning percentage.

By The Numbers

•••◯◯◯

New York Giants

F
O
O
T
B
A
L
L

Four players, Lawrence Taylor, Harry Carson, Mark Haynes and Dave Jennings were all selected to the Pro Bowl following the 1982 season despite New York's 4-5 record.

In the last game before the 1982 NFL strike, the Giants game against the Packers in Giants Stadium was marred by a power outage. However, Packers wide receiver James Lofton dealt the Giants a blow with 184 total yards and one touchdown. New York allowed 20-unanswered points in the second half and lost 19-27.

Bill Parcells was named Giants head coach after Ray Perkins resigned in 1982.

The Giants outscored their opponents 105-23 in the 1986 playoffs. The 82-point differential set an NFL record.

Amani Toomer gained a team-record 582 yards receiving in the postseason during his career with the Giants. He gained 136 yards on eight receptions against the 49ers in the 2002 Wild Card Playoffs.

Giants running back Rodney Hampton rushed for 1,182 yards in 1995, his fifth consecutive 1,000-yard season.

New York gained just 82-receiving yards against the Washington Redskins in the 1986 NFC Championship Game. This is the fewest yards gained for NY in a postseason game since 1950.

By The Numbers

• • • ○ ○ ○

New York Giants

○ ○ ○ ● ● ● —————————————————

F
O
O
T
B
A
L
L

On Oct. 28, 2007, the Giants and Dolphins played in the first regular-season NFL game played outside of North America. Over 80,000 fans packed Wembley Stadium in London, England, the second in the NFL's International Series. Both teams combined for 483 yards as a steady rain fell throughout the game. One highlight that got the attention of fans was a streaker who ran onto the field after halftime. Fans wore an array of shirts touting favorite NFL teams, college football teams and soccer teams, of course. Miami was the designated home team but trailed New York the entire game. The Giants won the game 13-10.

Carl Kinscherf punted 14 times for 583 yards against the Detroit Lions on Nov. 7, 1943, a Giants single-game record for punts and yardage. The game ended in a 0-0 tie. The Giants were limited to three first downs and 84 total yards while the Lions gained six first downs and 130 total yards.

Tiki Barber gained 5,183 receiving yards during his Giants career. He ranks third on the team's career list.

The Giants played 12 regular-season games at the Yale Bowl from October 1973 through the 1974 season. New York had a regular-season record of 1-11 at the Yale Bowl for a winning percentage of .083.

Bill Parcells led the Giants to a 3-12-1 record in 1983, his first season as the team's head coach.

By The Numbers

————————————————— ● ● ● ○ ○ ○

New York Giants

F
O
O
T
B
A
L
L

Homer Jones scored 13 receiving touchdowns and one rushing touchdown in 1967. His 84 total points scored led the Giants that season. He is the last receiver to lead the team in scoring for a season.

Frank Gifford scored 78 touchdowns, 10 PATs and two field goals during his career with the Giants. His 484 career points total is the highest in franchise history among non-kickers and places him third on the team's all-time list.

Phil McConkey had 84 fair catches on punt returns during his Giants career, a team career record.

Bill Parcells was named NFC East Coach of the Year in 1984 after leading the Giants to a 9-7 record.

Five Giants were named to the All-NFL Rookie Team in 1984.

Ali Haji-Sheikh's three field goals in the 1984 Wild Card Playoffs were the winning difference for the Giants. Even though NY was outgained by the Los Angeles Rams 192-214, the Giants won the game 16-13.

The 1984 NFC Divisional Playoffs marked the second postseason matchup between the Giants and 49ers. This second matchup wasn't much different from the first. The 49ers jumped out to a 21-10 halftime lead and both teams were held scoreless in the second half. NY was outgained 260-412 yards for the game.

By The Numbers

New York Giants

F
O
O
T
B
A
L
L

Kerry Collins had a .585 completion percentage as a Giant quarterback, the highest among Giant quarterbacks with at least 1,000 attempts. His lowest completion percentage was .568 in 2003; his highest was .615 in 2002 when he completed 335 of 545 attempts.

In 1985, the Giants posted the team's first back-to-back winning seasons in more than 20 years.

NY hosted a playoff game for the first time since 1962 when the Giants and 49ers faced off in the 1985 Wild Card Playoffs. The Giants didn't disappoint the 75,842 fans at Giants Stadium. Phil Simms' second quarter touchdown pass to Mark Bavaro gave New York a 10-0 advantage. Another Simms touchdown was the last score of the game. NY won 17-3.

New York and Chicago met in the 1985 NFC Divisional Playoffs. The Bears had the NFL's stingiest defense that season, and this game was much of the same. The Giants were shut out 0-21 and were outgained by a margin of more than 2-1. It was the third consecutive time the Giants were knocked out of the playoffs in the divisional round.

Featured Figure

Frank Gifford caught 17 passes for 236 yards in the postseason during his career with NY. His 13.9 yard average per reception in the postseason is highest in team history, edging out Amani Toomer's 13.8 yard average.

By The Numbers

New York Giants

F
O
O
T
B
A
L
L

The last time New York went undefeated at home was in 1986.

Kurt Warner had a Giants career quarterback rating of 86.5, the highest among quarterbacks with 250 or more career attempts. Warner completed 174 of 277 attempts for 2,054 yards, six touchdowns and four interceptions.

New York had a regular-season record of 2-5 at Shea Stadium in 1975 for a winning percentage of .286.

Phil Simms set a Giants single-season record in 1984 with 286 completed passes. The record would stand until broken by Kerry Collins in 2000.

After opening the 1986 season with a road loss to the Cowboys, New York won 14 of the next 15 games to finish first in the NFC East and tied for the best record in the league.

Bill Parcells was named NFL Coach of the Year in 1986.

Giants linebacker Lawrence Taylor was named NFL MVP in 1986.

New York faced the 49ers in the 1986 NFC playoffs for the third consecutive season. Phil Simms completed nine passes for four touchdowns. The 49ers turned the ball over four times, while NY played a nearly flawless game and beat San Francisco 49-3.

By The Numbers

••• ○○○

New York Giants

ooo••• ——————————————— 87

F
O
O
T
B
A
L
L

Giants defensive tackle Keith Hamilton returned a fumble 87 yards against the Kansas City Chiefs on Sept. 10, 1995. This is the longest fumble return in team history.

Amani Toomer returned a punt 87 yards for a touchdown against the Buffalo Bills on Sept. 1, 1996. This is a NY record for the longest punt return.

Rodney Hampton rushed for 187 yards against Dallas on Dec. 17, 1995. This was his highest single-game total with the Giants.

New York started the strike-shortened season of 1987 with five straight losses. Phil Simms threw just 17 touchdown passes, his lowest season total from 1984-88.

Fran Tarkenton led the NFL in 1969 with a passer rating of 87.2. He and Y.A. Tittle are the only Giants quarterbacks to have led the league in this category.

Tiki Barber scored on an 87-yard pass from Kent Graham against the Arizona Cardinals in 1998. This was Barber's longest reception as a Giant.

Featured Figure

Amani Toomer gained 608 yards receiving in the postseason during his career with the Giants, the most in team history. His total is almost more than the combined total of the second and third players ranked on the all-time list, Mark Bavaro (366) and Plaxico Burress (310).

By The Numbers

•••ooo

New York Giants

ooo•••

F
O
O
T
B
A
L
L

The Giants won 88 games in the 2000s, the most wins for the team in any decade.

New York's all-time record against the Detroit Lions in the regular season is 19-20-1, for a winning percentage of .488.

The Giants were eliminated from playoff contention in 1988 following a 21-27 loss to the Jets in Week 16, finishing 10-6 for the season.

The Giants gained just 288 yards and 23 touchdowns in a 31-3 win against the Chicago Bears in the 1990 NFC Divisional Playoffs. In contrast, the Bears had 11 first downs and 232 total yards.

Ahmad Bradshaw gained 88 yards on a rushing attempt against the Buffalo Bills on Dec. 23, 2007. This was the longest rushing attempt in the NFL that season and is the longest rush in Giants history that did not result in a score in an away game.

Bill Paschal rushed for 188 yards against the Redskins on Dec. 5, 1943. This stood as the Giants' single-game record until 1950.

Featured Figure

New York has played in the Pro Football Hall of Fame game four times, most recently against the Houston Texans in 2002. The Giants are 2-1-1 all time in this preseason game.

By The Numbers

•••ooo

New York Giants

○ ○ ○ • • •

89

F O O T B A L L

Amani Toomer wore jersey #89 his first two seasons with the Giants. In 1998 he switched to #81, the number he wore for the remainder of his Giants career.

Brad Daluiso had a field goal percentage of .889 in 1996, the highest in Giants history. He finished the season 24 of 27. Daluiso's percentage broke the record set by Ali Haji-Sheikh in 1983.

Dave Meggett gained 2,989 kickoff return yards during his career with the Giants. He ranks second on the team's all-time list.

The Giants played a back-and-forth game against the St. Louis Rams in the 1989 NFC Divisional Playoffs. New York scored six in the first and seven in the third, while St. Louis scored seven in the second and six in the fourth. In overtime, the Rams scored on a 30-yard pass from Jim Everett to Flipper Anderson to win the game.

Dave Meggett gained 582 yards on punt returns in 1989, a Giants single-season record. He broke the previous record set by Emlen Tunnell, who gained 489 yards in 1951. Meggett's season total ranks 25th of all time in NFL history.

Featured Figure

NY has an all-time regular-season record of 24-19 against current teams in the AFC West for a winning percentage of .558.

By The Numbers

• • • ○ ○ ○

New York Giants

○ ○ ○ ● ● ●

F
O
O
Tiki Barber led the league in yards-from-scrimmage in 2005 with 2,390 yards gained. This total also ranks third of all time in the NFL. He finished the season with 1,860 rushing yards and 530 receiving yards.

T
B
A
Rodney Williams kicked a 90-yard punt against the Denver Broncos on Sept. 10, 2001, the longest punt in NY history. It was the longest punt in the NFL that season and is the fourth longest in league history.

L
L
The Giants had a .900 winning percentage in 1929. This is the highest single-season winning percentage in team history. New York finished with a record of 13-1-1.

Leonard Marshall was named Defensive Player of the Week following the 1990 NFC Championship Game against the 49ers. He recorded four tackles, two sacks and two forced fumbles during the game. His sack of Joe Montana in the fourth quarter knocked the 49ers out of the game. Montana ended up with a fractured rib and bruised sternum following the sack by Marshall and later called this the hardest hit he ever took.

New York finished the 1990s with a regular-season record of 83-76-1 for a .522 winning percentage

The Giants have an all-time regular-season record at home of 349-240-16 for a .590 winning percentage.

By The Numbers

● ● ● ○ ○ ○

New York Giants

○ ○ ○ • • •

(91)

F
O
O
T
B
A
L
L

Domenik Hixon gained 1,291 kickoff return yards in 2009, a NY single-season record.

Hap Moran had a 91-yard rush against the Green Bay Packers on Nov. 23, 1930. This is the longest run from scrimmage in NY history that did not score.

The Giants have an all-time regular-season record of 359-246-16 at home for a winning percentage of .591.

Bill Parcells resigned as head coach of the Giants in May 1991. Giants offensive coordinator Ray Handley was announced as Parcells' replacement. New York finished 8-8 in Hadley's first season.

Giants kicker Lawrence Tynes made every PAT from 2008-10, going 91 for 91.

Dave Brown had 1,391 pass attempts in his career with NY. He ranks sixth of all time in this category.

Jeff Hostetler completed 28 of 34 pass attempts against Dallas on Sept. 29, 1991. His .824 completion percentage was the Giants' single-game record until 2002.

Featured Figure

On Sept. 15, 1968, Fran Tarkenton and Homer Jones hooked up for an 84-yard reception against the Pittsburgh Steelers. This is the longest pass play in Giants history that did not result in a touchdown.

By The Numbers

• • • ○ ○ ○

91

New York Giants

○○○•••————————————— **92**

FOOTBALL

Dave Jennings punted for 38,792 yards during his 11-year Giants career, a team record for career punt yardage. His total is 15,773 yards more than Don Chandler, whose career total is second on the Giants' career list.

New York finished 6-10 in 1992, the team's first losing season in five years.

Phil Simms had a passer rating of 92.7 in 1990, his career high. He had a career passer rating of 78.5.

Eddie Price gained 3,292 yards during his career with the Giants from 1950-55. He ranks eighth of all time in NY history.

Rodney Hampton scored a career high 14 touchdowns in 1992.

The Giants gained 192 first downs through the air in 2010. This is tied for fifth most passing first downs in a season in NY history.

Featured Figure

The Giants are one of just three NFL teams to have never had an official cheerleading squad. The Cleveland Browns and Detroit Lions are the other two teams. They are joined by the Chicago Bears, Green Bay Packers and Pittsburgh Steelers as the only current NFL teams without official cheerleaders.

By The Numbers

•••○○○

New York Giants

○ ○ ○ ● ● ●

F
O
O
T
B
A
L
L

Phil Simms fumbled the football 93 times during his career, a Giants record that ranks 19th on the NFL's all-time list in this category. He had six or more in 13 seasons.

Dan Reeves took over as head coach of the Giants in 1993. NY finished 11-5 and made the playoffs for the first time in three seasons. The Giants finished second to the Dallas Cowboys following a 13-16 overtime loss in Week 16.

New York head coach Dan Reeves was named NFL Coach of the Year by the Associated Press in 1993.

The Giants beat the Minnesota Vikings 17-10 in the 1993 Wild Card Playoffs thanks to a two-touchdown effort by Rodney Hampton in the third quarter.

The Giants defense ranked No. 1 in the NFL in 1993, giving up just 205 points during the regular season.

Eli Manning had a passer rating of 93.1 in 2009, his career high.

NY gained 93 yards on interceptions in 2002, the fewest yards gained since 1976.

Keith Hamilton led the Giants with 11.5 sacks in 1993. He finished his 12-year Giants career with 63.0 sacks.

By The Numbers

● ● ● ○ ○ ○

New York Giants

94

F
O
O
T
B
A
L
L

The Giants finished 9-7 in 1994 and missed the playoffs. It was the fourth time since 1970 that the Giants missed the playoffs with a winning record.

Ed Danowski led the NFL with 794 passing yards in 1935. He and Harry Newman are the only two Giants players to have led the league in this category.

The Giants gained 194 rushing yards against the Chicago Bears in 1990 Divisional Playoffs. This ranks third of all time in Giants postseason history, behind 216 yards gained against the 49ers in 1986 NFC Semifinals and 211 against the Browns in the 1958 Eastern Conference Playoffs.

Norm Snead completed a 94-yard pass to Rich Houston for a touchdown against the Cowboys on Sept. 24, 1972. This is the longest pass completion in a Giants regular-season home game.

Dave Brown started 15 games for the Giants in 1994. He completed 201 of 350 pass attempts for 2,536 yards with 12 touchdowns and 16 interceptions. The team finished 9-6 in his starts.

Featured Figure

Giants head coach Tom Coughlin played the position of wingback at Syracuse University. In 1967 he set a then school single-season receiving record.

By The Numbers

• • • ○ ○ ○

New York Giants

F
O
O
T
B
A
L
L

Phil Simms won 95 games as a starting quarterback, the most of any Giants quarterback. His overall record in New York was 95-64 for a .597 winning percentage.

Jim Fassel was named Coach of the Year by the Associated Press in 1997. The team finished 10-5-1 that season, the Giants' first winning season in four years.

Tiki Barber scored on a 95-yard rushing touchdown against the Oakland Raiders on Dec. 31, 2005, the longest running play in Giants history and the longest in the NFL that season.

New York lost seven games in 1995 on the last drive of the game. The team finished with a record of 5-11.

Joe Morrison had 395 career receptions with the Giants. He ranks third of all time in the category.

Rodney Hampton scored four rushing touchdowns against the New Orleans Saints on Sept. 24, 1995. This is the team record for the most touchdowns scored in a regular-season game.

Featured Figure

Giants kicker Bjorn Nittmo was the first Swedish-born player to play in the NFL. He played with the Giants in 1989, his only season in the NFL, making nine of 12 field goal attempts. While playing in New York, Nittmo appeared occasionally on *Late Night with David Letterman*.

By The Numbers

• • • ○ ○ ○

New York Giants

○○○ ●●● ──────────────── **96**

F
O
O
T
B
A
L
L

Tiki Barber led the league in yards-from-scrimmage in 2004 with 2,096 yards gained. He finished the season with 1,518 rushing yards and 578 receiving yards.

New York lost 0-24 to the Philadelphia Eagles on Dec. 1, 1996. This was the last time the Giants have been shut out.

New York's all-time regular-season record against the Washington Redskins is 91-61-4, for a winning percentage of .596.

The Giants finished 6-10 in 1996. It was the first time in 14 years that they had back-to-back losing seasons.

Dan Reeves was fired following the conclusion of the 1996 season.

Alex Webster carried the football 1,196 times from 1955-64. He was the first Giants player to have more than 1,000 career rushing attempts. He currently ranks fourth on the all-time list.

Joe Morris rushed for 5,296 yards in his career with the Giants. He was the first player to surpass 5,000 career rushing yards for New York.

Featured Figure

Jim Fassel is the most recent Giants head coach to win his first game. He led the Giants to a 31-17 victory over the Philadelphia Eagles on Aug. 31, 2004.

By The Numbers

●●● ○○○

96

New York Giants

○ ○ ○ • • •

F
O
O
T
B
A
L
L

97

Amani Toomer gained 9,497 receiving yards during his Giants career, a team record for the category. His total is more than 4,000 yards ahead of Frank Gifford, who is second on the list. Toomer ranks 38th on the NFL's career list for the most receiving yards.

Ron Dixon returned a third-quarter kickoff 97 yards for a touchdown against the Baltimore Ravens in Super Bowl XXXV. This was the only Giants touchdown for the game.

The last time a Giants game ended in a tie was on Nov. 23, 1997. New York tied the Washington Redskins 7-7.

The Giants finished in first place in the NFC East in 1997 after a last place finish the previous season. The team finished 7-0-1 in the division, the first team to go undefeated in NFC East Division play.

NY head coach Jim Fassel was named NFL Coach of the Year by *The Sporting News* in 1997.

Rodney Hampton surpassed Joe Morris' career rushing record in 1995. He finished with 6,897 and ranks second on NY's all-time list for the category.

NY rookie Ron Dixon returned the opening kickoff 97 yards for a touchdown in the 2000 NFC Divisional Playoff game against the Eagles. It was the only score of the quarter.

By The Numbers

• • • ○ ○ ○

97

New York Giants

○ ○ ○ ● ● ●

F
O
O
T
B
A
L
L

Y.A. Tittle had a .698 winning percentage as a starting quarterback, the highest among all Giant quarterbacks with at least 30 starts. His overall record was 32-13-3 from 1961-64.

Earl Morrall holds the Giants record for longest completed pass. He completed a 98-yard touchdown pass to Homer Jones in the fourth quarter against the Pittsburgh Steelers on Sept. 11, 1966. This was the second time that day the two players hooked up for a long touchdown pass. A 75-yard pass from Morrall to Jones in the first quarter gave the Giants an initial 7-0 lead. Morrall finished the day with 273 passing yards on 10 completions.

Giants running back Ron Johnson had 298 rushing attempts in 1972, the most in the NFL. He broke Eddie Price's record of 271 that was set in 1951. Hampton's record would stand for 15 seasons. Joe Morris broke it in 1986 with 341 attempts, who by the way is only surpassed by Tiki Barber's 357 in 2005.

Ron Johnson led the league in touchdowns scored that season with 14, nine rushing and five receiving.

Amani Toomer set a Giants record with a pass reception in 98 consecutive games from 1998-2004. Second on the list is Jeremy Shockey, who caught a pass in 83 consecutive games from 2002-07.

By The Numbers

● ● ● ○ ○ ○

New York Giants

99

F O O T B A L L

Phil Simms threw 199 touchdowns as a Giant, a team career record. He threw 11 or more touchdowns in 11 seasons and 21 or more in four different seasons.

Sean Landeta punted 16 times for 699 yards in New York's 1986 postseason games, an average of 43.7 yards per punt. The good field position throughout the postseason helped the Giants get to and win their first Super Bowl.

The Giants have an all-time regular-season record on the road of 277-278-17 for a .499 winning percentage.

In 1999, four players had more than 50 receptions each for the first time in NY history.

New York gained 399 yards against the Broncos in Super Bowl XXI, 263 passing yards and 136 rushing yards. This set a Giants record for the most total yards in a postseason game. This was later broken and currently ranks third.

Cary Blanchard made 15 of 21 field goal attempts in 1999. His .857 percentage made that season ranks third of all time among Giants players with 14 or more attempts.

Featured Figure

Charlie Conerly led the NFL in 1956 and 1959 with the lowest percentage of pass attempts intercepted. He is the only Giant to lead the league in this category more than once.

By The Numbers

• • • ○ ○ ○

New York Giants

○ ○ ○ ● ● ● ──────────────────

F
O
O
T
B
A
L
L

The Giants played their 500th game in team history on Nov. 14, 1965. New York lost that matchup 21-34 to the Cleveland Browns.

Bill Parcells had a winning percentage of .500 when coaching against the Giants. Parcells was 1-0 against New York with the Patriots, 0-1 with the Jets, and 4-4 with the Cowboys.

Benny Friedman led the Giants to a 2-0 record as a player-coach in 1930 for a perfect 1.000 winning percentage. He later coached the Brooklyn Dodgers football team to a 3-9 record in 1932.

Emlen Tunnell set a Giants record with a kickoff return of 100 yards against the New York Yankees football team in 1951. Clarence Childs matched this record against the Vikings in 1964.

New York finished the 2000s with a regular-season record of 88-72 for a .550 winning percentage.

The Giants game against Kansas City on Dec. 20, 1998, was the 1,000th game in NY history.

Steve Smith had 107 receptions for 1,220 yards in 2009. He is the only Giants receiver to have 100 or more receptions in a single season.

By The Numbers

● ● ● ○ ○ ○

*All information in this book is valid
as of the end of the
2010 season.*